Jordan:
A pilgrim's guide
by Bishop Sélim Sayegh

translated by Howard Curtis

ET REMOTISSIMA PROPE

Published by Hesperus Press Limited
4 Rickett Street, London sw6 1ru
www.hesperuspress.com

First published in Italy in 2003
Giordania: Guida del Pellegrino © Edizioni San Paolo s.r.l., 2003
English language translation © Howard Curtis, 2004
This translation first published by Hesperus Press Limited, 2004

Designed and typeset by Fraser Muggeridge
Printed in Jordan by Jordan National Press

isbn: 1-84391-903-6

Contents

Preface

This new book on the Jordan of the Old and New Testaments deals with a subject about which most people know little.

The different chapters, in presenting to us places mentioned in the Bible, juxtapose the cultural heritage of the Arab world with the roots of Christianity and even earlier, all of it an integral and important part of the story of salvation.

The author takes us through the various historical periods, introducing us to the Arameans, the Hebrews, the Moabites, the Edomites, the Nabataeans, and the populations of the Decapolis during the Greco-Roman period.

Guiding us on a virtual journey along the major routes of the period, he takes us to various places and shows us how a culture was developed in them which bore profound spiritual values and bestowed a gift on all mankind. Pre-Christian sites such as Ramtha, Mahanaim, Ma'in, Dhiban, Arnon, Rabba and Karak are mentioned; palaeo-Christian sites such as the place of Christ's baptism, Tabaqat Fahl, Umm Qais, Amman with the story of its martyrs, Madaba, Siyagha, Umm ar-Rasas and others.

For tourist and pilgrim alike, this book is a unique opportunity to become familiar with the monuments of Christian culture in a small but vibrant Arab country.

This book offers an essential overview which will be of use to visitors, without overburdening them with information. It illustrates not only the past, but what still remains in Jordan as a spiritual and human heritage for the country and for the whole world.

Jordan is part of the Holy Land, and therefore an essential destination for pilgrims. I am sure that they will find this book a travelling companion which throws light on the continuing history of Jordan, enriching tourists and pilgrims alike. This cultural nourishment is interwoven with a quest for the mysterious footsteps of God in the very places where he spoke.

Monsignor Michel Sabbah
Patriarch of the Latin Church of Jerusalem

Introduction

'Jordan, a land familiar to me from the Holy Scriptures'

On Monday March 20th, 2000, His Holiness John Paul II landed at Queen Alia airport in Amman, in an area called Zizia, in the Biblical territory of Moab, at the start of his pilgrimage to the holy places.

His twenty-seven hour visit to some of the holy places of Jordan took him through three regions known from the Bible: the land of Moab, the kingdom of the Ammonites and the land of Perea, also known as Trans-Jordan.

In his first speech, made soon after landing, His Holiness said:

Visit by King Abdullah and Queen Rania of Jordan to His Holiness John Paul II, the Vatican, September 22nd 1999. At this meeting, the king invited the Holy Father to visit Jordan during the Great Jubilee of the year 2000.

'Today I am in Jordan, a land familiar to me from the Holy Scriptures. A land sanctified by the presence of Jesus himself, the presence of Moses, Elijah, John the Baptist, and the martyrs and saints of the early Church.'

Every Christian who visits the holy places can experience the spiritual tension felt by the Holy Father. Every believer can return to their own country strengthened in grace, reinforced in piety and faith, stimulated in the love of the Word of God as revealed to them in the Holy Scriptures, and given help in improving their lives as Christians.

Part 1
The Biblical Nations in Jordan

Geographically speaking, Jordan occupies a position at the very heart of the Middle East, between Syria, Iraq, Saudi Arabia, Egypt, Palestine and Israel.

In ancient times, Jordan conquered many kingdoms and nations, was often passed through by travellers from other lands, and occupied a strategic position for trade. Aram, Ammon, Moab, Edom, Nabatea, the Decapolis, and Perea are the names that recur most often in the Bible.

Aram and Israel

Plain of the city of Ramtha, in northern Jordan, on the border with Syria, home of the Arameans.

The Arameans lived in the north of Jordan before the arrival of the Israelites in about the year 1200 BC. After the conquest, the tribes of Reuben and Gad settled in Madaba and Heshbon, while the tribe of

Cave used as a sepulchre, discovered in the vicinity of Ramtha.

Manasseh settled in the north of Jordan, on the mountains of Ajlun (Joshua 13:8–14 and 29–31; 17:1.).

The valley of the river Zarqa (Jabbok) separated the territory of this tribe from that of the Ammonites. Ramoth Gilead was situated on the north-western border and separated them from the Arameans of Damascus.

The second Book of Samuel tells how David attacked Hadadezer son of Rehob, the king of Zobah, who had come from the banks of the river

Euphrates to re-establish his own dominion.
The Arameans of Damascus came to the aid of
Hadadezer, but David killed 22,000 of them.
He then built a garrison in Damascus, making
the Arameans his subjects (2 Samuel 8:1–12).

After David and Solomon, Ramoth Gilead
(Ramtha) remained a disputed area because of its
strategic position along the major trade routes, and
Arameans and Israelites continued to fight for
control over it (1 Kings 20–22 and 2 Kings 6–7).

Ammon

According to the Book of Genesis, Lot's younger
daughter had a child to whom she gave the name
Ben-Ammi (son of my people) and who was the
father of the Ammonites (Genesis 19:38). During
the 13th century BC, the Ammonites settled on the
banks of the river Jabbok (Zarqa) and on the
surrounding mountains which join the outskirts
of Salt in the west to Heshbon in the south.

Deuteronomy 3:16–17 recalls that the Israelites
made no attempt to conquer Ammon, because of
this injunction:

'When you come near the land of the
Ammonites, do not trouble them or wage war
on them, for I will not give you possession of any
land of the children of Ammon; I have given it
to the descendents of Lot as a possession.'
(Deut 2:19)

Their capital was Rabbath Ammon (Amman).
Caravans on their way to Palestine and Damascus
passed through the city. This position was a source
of profit and a way of exercising influence over the
culture and faith of the surrounding nations. It is
said that the Ammonites built a series of towers to

Curious rocky
formation which
recalls the episode
in Genesis 19:26.

protect their little kingdom and keep watch on the caravan routes.

The Book of Judges tells us of a battle between the Ammonites and the Israelites, which took place after many years of oppression, as mentioned in these words:

> 'For eighteen years they persecuted and oppressed all the children of Israel who were on the east side of the Jordan in the land of the Amorites, which is Gilead.' (Judges 10:8)

Remains of the church in the monastery of Ain Abata, known as 'Lot's Cave'.

The Ammonites were later defeated by Jephthah the Gileadite, a mighty warrior who drove them out of the area, from the city of Aroer to the area around Minnith and as far as Abel Keramim (Judges 11:12–33).

The first Book of Samuel records the war waged by Nahash, king of the Ammonites, against Jabesh Gilead, and states that Saul came to the aid of the people of Jabesh and defeated the Ammonites (1 Samuel 11:1–11). The second Book of Samuel also refers to a war between David and the Ammonites (2 Samuel 10:1–11:1) during which Uriah the

Rugiun al-Malfouf, an Ammonite watchtower, on the caravan route. It dates from the seventh century BC and can be found in Amman.

Hittite, who had been placed in the front line on David's orders, met his death (2 Samuel 11:14–17). On that occasion, Joab, commander of the army of Israel, was unable to capture the city, which almost immediately regained its independence and prosperity.

David's son, King Solomon, would later marry an Ammonite woman, and allow her to worship her own gods, as related in 1 Kings 11:1–4.

Among the prophets who predicted doom and destruction for Rabbath Ammon were Amos (750 BC; cf. Amos 1:13), Jeremiah (c.625 BC; cf. Jeremiah 49:2) and Zephaniah (630 BC; cf. Zephaniah 2:8–10).

Many nations cast envious eyes on the little Ammonite kingdom, especially the great empires: the Assyrians (700–600 BC), the Babylonians (600–539 BC), the Persians (539–331 BC), the Greeks (331–63 BC) and the Romans (63 BC–636 AD).

It is worth recalling that under Ptolemy II, Rabbath Ammon was renamed Philadelphia, and the statue of Tyche, goddess of fortune, became the symbol of the good luck that Amman enjoyed over many centuries.

Tyche of Amman (goddess of good fortune), symbol of the autonomy given to the city. A marble sculpture from the Imperial era, second-third century BC. The crown is a symbol of the city.

With the conquest of Greece, the Roman Empire began to expand eastwards. In 63 BC, when the Roman legions, led by Pompey, occupied Palestine and Syria, the kingdom of the Ammonites was occupied and the city of Amman became part of the Decapolis.

Moab

The word *Moab* seems to be of Semitic origin. The etymology of the name ("who is his father") is a reference to Genesis 19:37, in which Lot's elder daughter gives birth to a son by her own father, a son who will become the ancestor of the Moabites.

The Holy Scriptures remain the principal source for information about Moab, its history and its borders. Its territory was bounded on the west by the Dead Sea, on the south by the valley of Sadim, on the east by the desert and on the north by the kingdom of the Ammonites. According to Numbers 22:1 and Deuteronomy 34:1, Moab also included the valleys between the Jabbok in the north and the Dead Sea, hence the name 'the plains of Moab'.

Ma'in (Baal Meon), 8 kilometres south-west of Madaba, in the territory of Moab.

During the 13th century BC, Moab was a prosperous kingdom with many towns and villages. The inhabitants cultivated the land and built fortresses along the eastern borders to protect themselves against incursions by tribes from the eastern desert.

Deuteronomy 2:9–11 states that when the Israelites, on their way towards Canaan, reached the border of the land of the Moabites, their king refused to let them pass. Moses did not attack them or challenge them to a battle, but instead preferred to bypass the land of Edom and Moab and go through the little kingdom of Heshbon on the plateau to the north of the river Arnon (Wadi Mujib).

The Book of Numbers (22:3–14) also recalls that the king of Moab, Balak son of Zippor, summoned Balaam to curse the Israelites. Despite the king's command, Balaam was forced to bless them.

Later, during the political upheavals which shook the whole region, Moab tried unsuccessfully to form a defensive alliance with the kingdom of Judah (cf. Isaiah 16:1–4). In the Book of Jeremiah (48:1–2, 18–19, 31–32), Jeremiah predicts the sad end for which Moab is destined.

Edom

Edom means 'red', recalling the name given to Esau, the son of Isaac, because of the colour of his hair (Genesis 25:25).

Located between the Dead Sea and the Gulf of Aqaba, on the eastern side of the valley of Wadi Araba, Edom was surrounded by the kingdoms of Judah in the west, Moab in the north, the desert in the east, and Egypt and the Red Sea in the south.

Ancient Egyptian chronicles state that during the time of the twelfth dynasty (2000–1788 BC), the area

View of Wadi Araba (from Ras al-Nagab) in the land of Edom.

was called Seir and was inhabited by the Horites (Genesis 14:6). They were expelled when the descendents of Esau took possession of the region (Deuteronomy 2:12).

Although Edom was largely arid desert, its inhabitants practised agriculture and trade and mined copper and iron. The kingdom acquired great importance because of its privileged position on the 'Kings' Highway' which joined Egypt to present-day Jordan, Palestine, Syria and Iraq.

The ruins discovered so far demonstrate that the

culture of the Edomites flourished during the 13th century BC and continued until the 6th century BC. Like the Moabites, they built great fortresses to protect their borders. Their tribes (Genesis 36:15–19) gradually organised themselves and elected a king, before the monarchy had been established in Israel (Genesis 36:31–43).

Even though the Hebrews considered them, in many ways, their 'brothers', the Edomites were nevertheless a hostile power. When Saul became king of Israel, he fought the Moabites, the Ammonites and the Edomites (1 Samuel 14:47). David did the same when he became king, defeating them and making them his subjects (1 Chronicles 18:13). His son Solomon kept a fleet at Ezion Geber, near Eilat, on the Red Sea, in the territory of Edom (1 Kings 9:26).

According to 2 Kings 3:9–27 the Edomites formed an alliance with Israel and Judah to combat Mesha, king of Moab, an alliance which ended in failure. The Edomites rebelled against Jehoram, king of Judah (848–841 BC) who was unable to wipe them out (2 Kings 8:20–22). They were defeated by Amaziah, a later king of Judah (811–782 BC) near the valley of Salt. He occupied their capital, Sela, (2 Kings 14:7), and, according to the second Book of Chronicles (25:14), committed an act which displeased the Lord: he carried off the idols of Seir and made them his gods, worshipping them and offering them sacrifices.

When Nebuchadnezzar became king of Babylon, he immediately tried to extend his kingdom westwards. After defeating the Egyptians at Carchemish in 605 BC, he turned his attention to Jerusalem, which he conquered in 587 BC. Its inhabitants were deported to Babylon as slaves. Psalm 137:7 reminds us that the Edomites rejoiced

at what had happened and seized the opportunity
to occupy the city of Hebron, which remained under
their control until Judas Maccabeus retook it in the
second century BC. Only when John Hyrcanus, son
of Simon Maccabeus, became leader of the army in
142 BC did the Edomites assimilate with the Jews
and agree to be circumcised.

The kingdom of Edom, according to the Book
of Jeremiah, was also noted for its wise rulers. Elifaz
of Teman, one of the wisest of Job's friends, was an
Edomite (Job 2:11).

Among the Edomites in the New Testament,
mention should be made of Herod and the crowds
who followed Jesus when he withdrew into the
desert (Mark 3:8). The Edomite language was
similar to Hebrew.

The kingdom of the Nabataeans

The Nabataeans were originally nomads from the
Arabian peninsula. In the sixth century BC they
settled in Petra, living in peace with the inhabitants
of the region, the Edomites, whom they
subsequently supplanted. The Shara mountains soon
became the heart of their kingdom, which extended,
in its period of greatest splendour, as far as the
Hejaz in the south-east, the Red Sea in the south,
the Mediterranean in the west and Damascus in
the north.

As traders, they benefited from their
geographical position at the crossroads of the
great trading routes. They prospered thanks to
the caravans that crossed their territory, building
fortified cities to ensure their safety, supplying the
roads with water, and demanding tolls from those
who passed, from whom they bought and resold
goods. The most famous part of the kingdom of the

Al-Sharah, a range of mountains near Petra, from which Dushara, the principal god of Petra, took his name.

Nabataeans is Petra, a city carved out of the rocks.

The golden age of the Nabataeans as a trading nation was the second century BC. It was during this period that they also developed agriculture and irrigation systems, and built dams and wells to take the best possible advantage of the low rainfall.

In the Hellenistic period (333–63 BC), neither the Ptolemites nor the Seleucids ever managed to conquer them. Antigonus, one of the commanders of Alexander the Great (306–301 BC) sent his troops to conquer Petra, but failed.

At first, the Jews had good relations with the Nabataeans: 1 Maccabees 5:25 records the welcome extended by the Nabataeans towards Judas Maccabeus and his brother Jonathan, who had fled from Bacchides across the wilderness of Thecoe. This understanding is confirmed in 1 Maccabees 9:35, when Jonathan sent his brother John 'to ask his friends the Nabataeans if they could leave with them their belongings, which were numerous.' On that occasion, however, the sons of Jambri ambushed John near Madaba and seized him, along with all his belongings. The good relations between the Nabataeans and Maccabeans came to an end when the latter captured the gate of Gaza, threatening Nabataean commercial interests.

In 93 BC, war broke out in Gadara (Umm Qais), between Obodas I, king of the Nabataeans, and Alexander Jannaeus, king of Judah. The Jews were defeated, and the Nabataeans conquered the south of Syria (presently northern Jordan and the mountains of al-Druz). A few years later, in 85 BC, Obodas also defeated the Seleucids, led by Antiochus II, in a battle in the Negev desert. Antiochus died, his army was dispersed, and Damascus fell under Nabataean dominion for a time.

Petra.
Columned street from
the Roman period.

Tensions resurfaced in the time of Herod Antipas, when he divorced his first wife, the daughter of the king of the Nabataeans, to marry Herodias, the wife of his brother Philip. These tensions, in fact, lasted a long time, because the Romans hampered the commercial interests of the Nabataeans and their very existence: it was the emperor Trajan who would finally defeat them, joining their territory with that of Bostra in Syria to form a new province of the Empire: the province of Arabia.

The Nabataean civilisation survived, but from that point its style became pure Roman.

There had been a Christian presence in Petra since the beginnings of Christianity. With the end of the persecutions, in the fourth century, it would become a Christian city and an archbishopric.

Both Petra and the surrounding towns seem to have been destroyed in an earthquake in 743–748 AD.

Bronze coins minted in the Roman period for the cities of the Decapolis.

Coin minted for the city of Abila.

Coin minted for the city of Gerasa.

The Decapolis

The Roman general Pompey conquered Syria in 63 BC. In the same year he laid siege to Jerusalem and captured it, crushing all resistance. The Jewish State came under the power of the Romans, who reorganised the administrative and political affairs of the whole region, encouraging the autonomy of ten cities, among them Gaza, Jamnia, Ashdod and Jaffa, on the Mediterranean coast. To the people of Israel they left Judea, the western part of Edom to the west of the Dead Sea, Perea and Galilee. When the Jews later supported Julius Caesar against Pompey, they were given back Jaffa and the plains of Sharon, while Samaria retained its autonomy.

The name Decapolis (a Greek word meaning 'Ten cities') refers to the region between Damascus and Philadelphia (Amman) and the alliance between ten cities established by Pompey when he conquered the region. The Romans wanted these Hellenistic cities to form a union, not only to defend their own borders, but also to preserve their culture and traditions from Hebrew influence. The alliance was based on a system of administrative autonomy similar to that which our mayors have today. Each city included the surrounding villages and countryside linked to them. They had to pay a tribute to the Roman governor of Syria.

Coin minted for the city of Hippos.

The Gospels often mention the Decapolis. Matthew refers to large crowds from the Decapolis and the regions beyond Jordan who followed Jesus (cf. Matthew 4:25), while Mark writes that Jesus 'left the vicinity of Tyre and went from Sidon to the sea of Galilee, through the territory of the Decapolis', where he healed a deaf-mute (cf. Mark 7:31–37). Previously, in the territory of Gerasa, he had freed a man possessed by evil spirits who had then spread the news throughout the Decapolis of what Jesus had done for him (cf. Mark 5:20).

Coin minted for the city of Capitolias.

Coin minted for the city of Capitolias.

The historian Flavius Josephus (27–75 AD) briefly refers to the alliance of the ten cities, but does not record their names. The famous Roman writer Pliny (62–113 AD), on the other hand, records the entire list. The cities were Damascus, Dibon, Philadelphia (Amman), Abila, Scythopolis (Beisan), Gadara (Umm Qais), Pella (Tabaqat Fahl), Hippos, Gerasa (Jerash) and Canatha. All the cities mentioned, with the exception of Scythopolis, are in the region to the east of the river Jordan, and seven of them are in Jordan.

Coin minted for the city of Philadelphia.

In the second century AD, Ptolemy increased the number of cities in the alliance to eighteen; one of

Coin minted for the city of Pella.

the new cities was Capitolias. This did not, however, entail either a change of name or a change of borders.

Coin minted for the city of Durun.

Perea

Perea is the name given to the region to the east of the river Jordan. It is a strip of land thirty-five kilometres wide and about a hundred kilometres from north to south, extending from the town of Pella, southwards to the mountains of Salt, on the eastern shore of the Dead Sea, and as far as the fortress of Machaerus and the valley of the river Arnon. It is bordered by the Decapolis to the north, the Decapolis and the kingdom of the Ammonites to the east, the kingdom of the Nabataeans to the south, and Samaria and Judea in the west.

Coin minted for the city of Scythopolis.

At the time of Jesus, Perea, like Galilee, was ruled by Herod Antipas, son of Herod the Great. Jesus called him a 'fox' (cf. Luke 13:31–32). Matthew states that many people from this region followed Jesus (Matthew 4:25) and brought him their sick to cure. This is confirmed by Mark, who records how Jesus, after curing a man with a shrivelled hand on the Sabbath (Mark 3:1–6), withdrew to the region of the sea with his disciples.

Coin minted for the city of Gadara.

> 'From Judea', and from Jerusalem, from Idumea, from the territory beyond the Jordan (Perea), and from around Tyre and Sidon, many people came to him when they heard all things he was doing.' (Mark 3:8)

Coin minted for the city of Gadara.

According to the fourth Gospel, John the Baptist was performing baptisms in Bethany beyond the Jordan, when the Jews of Jerusalem sent him priests and Levites to ask him: 'Who are you?' It was there that five of his disciples joined Jesus and he started

his public ministry. This 'Bethany beyond the
Jordan' would remain a place of escape and refuge
for Jesus at particularly difficult times (cf. John
10:40).

View of the territory of
Perea, corresponding
to the Old Testament
region of Gilead.

The capital of Perea was Gadara (Tell al-Jadur),
a village near Salt, not to be confused with the much
more famous Gadara (Umm Qais) of the Decapolis.
Roman ruins, columns and enormous rocks were
found there, which the inhabitants, heedless of their
historical value, re-used to build houses.

There are no doubt still many Christian ruins
buried underground; recently, two cemeteries have
been identified, one of them in a wooded valley in a
place called Sara. Many copper coins have also been
unearthed, among them one bearing the effigy of
King Herod Agrippa (37–44 AD) and another that
of the emperor Constantine I (306–337 AD).

Perea also has a connection with John the
Baptist. According to the account of Flavius

Josephus, when John was arrested by Herod, he was imprisoned and martyred in the fortress of Machaerus (cf. Mark 6:17–29).

International trade routes

When we speak of trade routes in the context of the Old Testament, we must forget all our contemporary images of cars, trains, planes, asphalt roads, and immerse ourselves in a world of camels, horses and donkeys, which were the only vehicles in use at that time.

Two great roads feature particularly in the Old Testament:

The King's Highway, which is mentioned in the Book of Numbers. This road started in Egypt, passed through the Sinai desert, and entered Jordan at Aqaba/Eilat. From there it headed north to Petra, Karak, Ara'ir, Heshbon and Amman. From Amman it continued northwards through Gerasa, Ramoth Gilead (Ramtha) and Damascus, until it reached the Caspian Sea. Many secondary roads branched out from it, linking the surrounding towns and villages. Moses and the Israelites took this route on their journey towards the land of Canaan, until they reached the land of Edom, where the inhabitants blocked their progress (cf. Numbers 20:14–18).

Milestone discovered along the Sea Road.

The Sea Road, referred to by Isaiah in these words:

> 'In the past, he disgraced the land of Zebulun and the land of Naphtali, but in the future he will honour Galilee of the nations, by way of the sea, beyond the Jordan.' (Isaiah 9:1)

This road ran from the north of Egypt, on the shores of the Mediterranean, as far as Gaza, where it then divided into two.

One branch ran alongside the sea, while the other went into the territory of Palestine. The two branches joined up again at Aphek and from there continued towards Damascus, Hamah and Aleppo. Numerous secondary arteries also branched off from these two roads.

These roads were not only essential for the economy, but were much used by armies in times of war, as the history of the Egyptians, the Assyrio-Babylonians and the Arameans clearly shows.

Each kingdom was greatly concerned about the safety of its own roads. When people set off on trading expeditions, they usually travelled in groups, forming caravans to protect themselves from possible bandits.

In the first century AD, the emperor Trajan (52–117) ordered the King's Highway to be renovated. His successor Hadrian (117–138 AD) inaugurated the new road during a visit to the region, an occasion which also saw the building of the triumphal arch at Gerasa.

The pilgrim Egeria (394 AD) writes of having visited the region using the road that goes from Jerusalem to Jericho, and then from Jericho to Heshbon, passing through Rama (called Livias). Milestones marking the fifth, sixth and seventh miles of the King's Highway can still be seen today in the vicinity of Heshbon.

Part II

The most important biblical sites and Christian ruins in Jordan

Jordan is a vast open-air archaeological museum, with more than nine thousand historical sites, which are constantly being enriched with new discoveries. The present guide only deals with the most important Old Testament towns and the principal Christian ruins. We shall proceed from north to south, beginning with the northern cities, continuing with the sites in the central regions, and finally moving south to end with the holiest place in all Jordan: the area of Jesus' baptism and the site of Bethany beyond the Jordan.

Ramoth Gilaead (Ramtha)

The Bible mentions a city in Jordan located on the border between Israel and the kingdom of the Arameans (present-day Syria). It was an important centre, positioned on the main trade routes, which in ancient times was called Ramoth Gilead.

Archaeologists and experts believe that Ramoth Gilead corresponds to the present day Tell al-Ramith, five kilometres south of Ramtha. It is most likely the name Ramtha itself derives from Ramoth.

The city of Ramoth is mentioned in Deuteronomy 4:43 and Joshua 20:8 as a city of refuge for those who had unintentionally committed murder. In a society where vendettas were rife, it was important to ensure that there were places

where such people could continue to live without
fear, while awaiting judgement.

The name of the city goes back to the times of
King Solomon (972–933 BC) who appointed twelve
commissioners to take turns at supplying the court
with food for a month. Among them we find a
certain Ben-Geber, who was appointed prefect of
Ramoth Gilead (cf. 1 Kings 4:13). During the reign
of Omri (886–875 BC), the city fell into the hands
of the Arameans. Later, the Israelites defeated the
enemy troops at Aphek (cf. 1 Kings 20:26–34) but
were unable to retake the city. Ahab (875–853 BC)
made another attempt, rejecting the previous peace
treaty, and trying to enlist the help of Jehoshaphat,
king of Judah (870–846 BC) to retake the city. On
the occasion of a visit by Jehoshaphat to Samaria,
Ahab said to him:

> 'Do you not know that Ramoth Gilead belongs
> to us, and yet we have done nothing to take it out
> of the hands of the king of Aram? And he asked
> Jehoshaphat: Will you go with me to attack

Ramoth Gilead
(Ramtha), on the
northern border
between Jordan and
Syria. The city was for
a long time fought
over by the kingdoms
of Aram and Israel.

Ramoth Gilead.
Roman-era tombs.

Ramoth Gilead? And Jehoshaphat answered the king of Israel, I am as you are, my people as your people, my horses as your horses.' (1 Kings 22:3–4)

But Ahab died in battle (1 Kings 22:29–37) and Ramoth Gilead remained in the hands of the Arameans until it was recaptured by other kings. Ahab's son Joram was also wounded in battle in an attempt to defend Ramoth Gilead (cf. 2 Kings 8:28).

It was here that a disciple of the prophet Elisha anointed Jehu, king of Israel, with the support of the army. Pouring oil on his head, he said: 'I anoint you king over the Lord's people Israel. And you shall destroy the house of Ahab your master.' (2 Kings 9:6–7)

During the reign of Jehoahaz (820–803 BC), Hazael, king of Aram, recaptured Ramoth, humiliating the Israelites and making them pay substantial taxes. On that occasion, the king of Israel was left with only fifty horsemen, ten chariots and ten thousand foot soldiers (cf. 2 Kings 13:3–7).

Gadara (Umm Qais)

Gadara was one of the cities of the Decapolis. It is
not known how, or when, the name came to be
changed.

Gadara began to flourish under Greek influence,
after Alexander the Great's conquest of the East,
in particular after the reign of the Seleucid king
Antiochus III (223–186 BC), who was much disliked
by the Jews. It was during his reign that the
Maccabees rebelled against the Hellenistic yoke,
which they regarded as having tainted the identity
of Israel. They occupied many cities in Gilead,
destroying all signs of Hellenistic culture. Gadara
was one of the cities which was attacked, and its
inhabitants were put to the sword.

Gadara (Umm Qais):
basilica with a central
octagonal plan. The
original paving of
the ambulatory
surrounding the
octagon has been
preserved.

When the Romans conquered Syria and Palestine, they removed the cities of the Decapolis from Jewish political influence and turned them into a league of 'independent cities'. For Gadara, this was a period of great peace and prosperity. The Roman historian Strabo (106–44 BC) writes:

> 'The Romans, who like to enjoy themselves, after being at the baths of Hammath, emerge to refresh their spirits on the heights of Gadara and spend their time watching spectacles in its theatres.'

The ruins of a large church and two theatres have been unearthed in Gadara. Restoration work on the theatre adjacent to the church has made it possible for the visitor to go back in time: he can take his place on one of the stone seats, as thousands of people did over the centuries, and enjoy the enchanting view of the Golan Heights, Lake Tiberias and Mount Tabor.

Gadara (Umm Qais). Roman-era statue.

Many tombs have also been found in Gadara, valued for their architectural refinement. One of them bears this inscription:

> 'This I say to you, passer-by: I was once as you are, and you will be as I am, so treat life as a mortal should.'

According to Mark's Gospel, Jesus crossed Lake Tiberias into the region of the Gadarenes, where he met a man who lived in the caves and was possessed by a legion of demons. After Jesus had cured him, the demons entered a herd of pigs, which then ran into the lake. The keepers of the pigs ran to tell everyone what had happened, and the citizens of Gadara came out to meet Jesus and begged him to leave their city (cf. Mark 5:1–17).

History records several noteworthy figures from Gadara, among them the poet Meleager, who moved to Tyre in 110 BC, and then to the island of Kos and to Rome, and the Epicurean philosopher and poet Philodemus. Many of the latter's writings have been discovered in the Italian city of Herculaneum, which was destroyed in the eruption of Vesuvius in 79 AD.

Among the Christian personalities, mention should be made of Bishop John, who participated in the council of Chalcedon in 451 AD, and Deacon Zacharias, martyred during the persecutions authorised by the emperor Diocletian in the fourth century.

Capitolias (Beit Ras)

Capitolias (Beit Ras), about five kilometres north of Irbid, was another of the cities of the Decapolis, and had a period of great prosperity. The scattered ruins date from the Roman and Byzantine periods. The present-day village grew up on the remains of the old city, the stones of whose temples and churches were re-used to build houses. The ruins

Capitolias (Beit Ras). The new town. There are caves and tombs from the Roman-Byzantine era hidden in the surrounding hills, which are used today as stables or barns.

Capitolias (Beit Ras).
Main street (cardo)
of the city.

of two churches can still be seen, one of them dedicated to the Virgin Mary. It was in the latter that the holy martyr Peter officiated in the eighth century.

Another bishop of Capitolias was Antiochus, who participated in the council of Nicea in 325 AD and added his signature to its documents. Two other eminent figures linked to the city were Bishop Ananias, who took part in the council of Chalcedon in 451 AD, and bishop Theodorus, who participated in the synod of Jerusalem in 536.

Abila

The city of Abila is mentioned by the Latin writer and naturalist Pliny (23–79 AD), in his book *Historia naturalis*. In it he declares: 'Abila is one of the cities of the Decapolis, situated near Gadara and Capitolias.' It is important not to confuse it with the Abila in Perea, near Livias, which is mentioned by the famous geographer Ptolemy in the second century AD.

Abila. Columns of the fifth-century cross-shaped basilica.

As in all the principal Roman cities, Abila bears the marks of a pleasure-loving civilisation: theatres, temples, streets, a forum. The Roman theatre is still visible, as are the remains of the public baths slightly further to the east.

There was a strong Christian presence in the city from the end of the fourth century AD. Three churches have recently been discovered, dating from the fifth and sixth centuries, including a fifth-century cross-shaped basilica in the southern part of the ruins, beautifully carved out of basalt. There is also a fourth church, smaller in size, dating from the seventh century.

The shrine of the phophet Elijah

The ruins of the shrine of the Prophet Elijah can be found about ten kilometres north of Ajlun, roughly 900 metres above sea level. Christians have always shown great devotion to the prophet Elijah, the man who embodied the first commandment: 'You shall have no other God but me.'

A church from the Byzantine period has recently been discovered, covering a surface area of about 1340 square metres. It was built between the sixth and seventh centuries, as the dedicatory inscription found on the southern portico of the church records:

> 'The priest, the presbyter Saba, and his wife generously gave this work to the holy Church and the prophet Elijah in 622.'

Hilltop with the great complex of the shrine dedicated to the prophet Elijah, who according to tradition was born here.

In front of the entrance was a semi-circular uncovered courtyard, reached by a staircase on its west side. Part of this staircase can still be seen. Among the finds in the area have been pieces of marble, the altar, some oil lamps, and a few coins

dating from the time of Constantine II (541–568 AD). Detail of the mosaics in the shrine of the prophet Elijah.

The veneration of Elijah is linked to the prophet's birthplace, about a kilometre to the northwest, in the village of Listib. It is in the first Book of Kings that we find this brief allusion to Elijah's birthplace:

'Now Elijah, from Tishbe in Gilead, said to Ahab, As the Lord God of Israel lives, whom I serve, there will be neither dew nor rain in these years, except at my word.' (1 Kings 17:1)

Tishbe in Gilead is the present-day Listib. The Bible continues:

'And the word of the Lord came to Elijah, saying, Leave this place, and turn eastward, and hide by the brook of Cherith, east of the Jordan. And you will drink from the brook; and I have commanded the ravens to feed you there. And he did as the Lord had said, and went and dwelt by the brook Cherith, east of the Jordan. And the ravens brought him bread and meat in the morning, and bread and meat in the evening; and he drank from the brook.' (1 Kings 17:2–6)

The river Cherith is today called Wadi al-Yabis

(dry valley). It is a surprising name, given that the valley is not at all 'dry'. On the contrary, the area is a fertile one, with spectacular landscapes. Its original name was more appropriate: Wadi Elias.

The birthplace of Jephthah of Gilead

The area around Ajlun was the birthplace of Jephthah of Gilead, one of the key characters in the Book of Judges. The history of Ajlun goes much further back than the era of the Judges. Ceramics and other finds in the area suggest that Ajlun was inhabited as long ago as the first Bronze Age (1900–1550 BC), and probably enjoyed great strategic and commercial importance because of its geographical position.

The Book of Judges offers us a glimpse of the life of the tribes of Israel in the least known period of their history (1200–1000 BC), before the establishment of the monarchy.

Jephthah of Gilead lived towards the end of the 12th century BC. According to the scriptures, this was a period when the children of Israel turned their backs on the Lord and worshipped the Baals and the Astartes, the gods of Aram, Sidon and Moab, the gods of the Ammonites and the Philistines. Jephthah was a valiant warrior. He was born out of wedlock, and when he grew up he was rejected by his relatives with these words: 'You will not inherit anything in our father's house.' (Judges 11:2) Jephthah fled from his family to the land of Tob, in the territory between Dira and Damascus. There he fell in with bad company, and went around with them. It was at this time that the Ammonites, crossing the Jordan, fought the tribes of Judah, Benjamin and Ephraim, and established their camp in Gilead. The men of Gilead gathered at Mizpah (Anjara) to confront

the enemy, but they were afraid and lacked a valiant commander. They decided to summon Jephthah from the land of Tob, with the words: 'Come, and be our commander, so that we can fight the children of Ammon.' (Judges 11:6) Jephtha tried to wriggle out of it, but in vain. He led his troops, supported by the soldiers of Manasseh, from Mizpah into Ammonite territory, making the following promise to God:

> 'If you deliver the children of Ammon into my hands, then whatever comes out of the door of my house to meet me, when I return in victory from the children of Ammon, will be the Lord's, and I will offer it up as a burnt offering.' (Judges 11:30–31)

Jephthah was victorious in the battle and crushed the Ammonites confronting Israel. When he returned to his house in Mizpah, his daughter came out to greet him, dancing and playing the cymbals. Although she was his only daughter, he kept his

Cave still known as 'Jephthah's cave', near Ajlun, northern Jordan.

promise and offered her as a burnt offering. Today, there is still a cave near Ajlun which bears his name.

In the 1950s, some mosaics were found in a house near the Latin church of Ajlun, as well as walls of ancient houses, arches and ceramics from the Roman and Byzantine periods in the market district.

In 1998, a complex of buildings was discovered in the Biddiah area, including a church dating from the fifth or sixth century AD, with a polychrome mosaic floor. In another part of the town, the remains of a large church from the sixth century have been unearthed. Here, too, there is a mosaic floor, although it is badly damaged.

Ajlun is also famous for its castle, which is generally thought to have been built by Izz ad-Din Usama in 1185 AD on the ruins of a Byzantine monastery. After the period of the Crusades, the castle was abandoned, and in 1837 was badly damaged by an earthquake.

Excavations in a high room of the castle have brought to light a small chapel covered with mosaics. Between two eagles, disfigured by iconoclasts, there is a short inscription which has made it possible to

Ajlun. The castle built on the ruins of the Byzantine monastery.

Ajlun. Detail of the
castle interior.

date the decoration to a period before the eighth
century.

In Ajlun, as in the surrounding towns and
villages, artistic and historical treasures still remain
buried, awaiting a coordinated campaign of
archaeological excavations, under government
supervision, using the latest scientific methods.

Anjara

The city of Anjara is situated south of Ajlun, and
is probably the Mizpah mentioned in the Old
Testament (cf. for example Judges 11:29–34). So far,
there has not been any archaeological research done
on the town, and all its treasures remain buried.

As Anjara is in the territory of the Decapolis, it is
reasonable to conjecture that Jesus may have passed
through it and performed one of his miracles here
(cf. Matthew 8:28–34; Mark 7:31–37).

Thirty years ago, at a time when it was impossible for the Christians of Jordan to go on a pilgrimage to the holy places in Jerusalem and Bethlehem because of the Israeli occupation of Palestine, a sanctuary was built in Anjara, dedicated to Our Lady of the Mountain.

Mahanaim

The name Mahanaim means 'two camps' (from mahna, meaning 'camp'). Situated north of Ajlun, in an area of great natural beauty, the city appears for the first time in the Book of Genesis:

> 'And Jacob went on his way, and the angels of God met him. And when Jacob saw them, he said, This is God's camp: and he named that place Mahanaim.' (Genesis 32:1–3)

Mahanaim. It was here that King David found refuge during the attempt by his son Absalom to usurp the throne.

The city returns to centre stage in the history of Israel as the scene of a tragic episode, narrated in the second Book of Samuel: the attempt by David's son Absalom to usurp his father's throne. Informed of the conspiracy by a spy, David left Jerusalem and fled north to the other side of the Jordan, along the

road leading to Mahanaim. When David arrived there, Absalom crossed the Jordan with all the men of Israel, and settled in Gilead to prepare for the decisive battle. The battle was fought in the forests of Mahanaim (2 Samuel 18:6). Absalom was riding on a mule when he passed beneath a large oak tree and his hair was caught in the branches, so that he was left hanging in mid-air, while the mule continued on its way. David's general, Joab, plunged three spears into his heart, then left the task of killing him to ten of his young armour-bearers (2 Samuel 18:7–17).

Jerash

The city of Jerash has been inhabited since the Bronze Age, as is proved by the caves situated to the north-east of the city. It was subject to all the social and political changes that affected the region, and had a period of great prosperity during the reign of Ptolemy III (246–221 BC). It was later captured by the Jewish leader Alexander Jannaeus (102–76 BC) and remained under Jewish domination until it was liberated by the Roman legions led by Pompey, towards the middle of the first century AD. He assigned it to the Province of Syria, and made it one of the cities of the Decapolis.

The Romans made it a model city, architecturally and socially. The architects achieved remarkable results in building and layout. In accordance with the Roman style, the main street was the heart of the city, with columns on either side. This street was crossed by two other thoroughfares, thus allowing a free flow of traffic throughout the city. At the end of the northern artery an inscription has been found which dates the walls of the city to 75–76 AD. In the centre of the city was the great horseshoe-shaped

Jerash. Main street of the city, with columns on either side. The staircase leading to the temple of the goddess Artemis is clearly visible.

market square, which was paved and surrounded by tall columns.

When the emperor Hadrian visited Jerash in the winter of 129–130 AD, the population built a triumphal arch in his honour.

There are an enormous number of columns and temples in Jerash. The most famous temples are those to Artemis, from 162 AD, and Zeus, which took more than fifty years to build. The Temple of Artemis can be reached from the main street by way of a staircase more than eighty metres long, lined by columns. Besides the temples, the city contained large baths and two theatres.

So far, about twenty churches have been found in Jerash. The most important of these, and probably

also the oldest, is the cathedral, which was built
in the middle of the fourth century AD. The most
important Christian celebration in the city was the
one commemorating the miracle of Cana in Galilee,
when the fountain in the western courtyard of the
cathedral was filled with wine and everybody was
allowed to drink from it. The church of Saint
Theodore was built in the vicinity of the cathedral
in 494–496, and another three churches were built
further to the west between 529 and 533 AD. The
central one is dedicated to John the Baptist, and
those on either side to Saint George and Saints
Cosmas and Damian. There are connecting doors
between the three churches.

Jerash. Theatre discovered in the southern area of the excavations.

In the eastern part of the city are the remains of
a church known as the 'church of Procopius', after
the army officer who built it at his own expense in
526–527 AD. Another church, dedicated to Saints
Peter and Paul, can be found to the south west.

Various inscriptions have been found which
record the names of the city's bishops: Exerecius

(359 AD), Planco (431 AD), Claudius (464 AD), Eneus
(496 AD), Paul (526–534 AD), Anastasius (after
Bishop Paul), Isaias (559 AD), Marianus (570 AD)
and Genesius (611 AD).

Shaken by strong earthquakes, in particular that
of 747 AD, the city underwent much rebuilding in the
course of its history.

Beth Rehob (Rihab beni Hassan)

Twenty-six kilometres from Jerash, on the road to
Mafraq, is the site of the Biblical city of Beth Rehob.
It is mentioned in 2 Samuel 10:6, which tells how,
to strengthen his army, the king of the Ammonites
hired twenty thousand men from among the
Arameans of Beth Rehob and Zobah, and sent them
to attack David's army. Many scholars believe that
the Beth Rehob of 2 Samuel 10:6 and the Rehob
mentioned in Numbers 13:21 and Judges 18:28 are
in fact one and the same place: Rihab beni Hassan.

Rihab Beni Hassan.
One of the fifteen
churches found in
the excavations of
the city.

The most important Christian ruins in Rihab are the many churches: the church of Saint Mary (534 AD); the church of Saint Paul (596 AD) with its three naves and geometric mosaics; the Church of Saint Sophia (604 AD); the church of Saint Stephen (620 AD); the church of Saint Peter, constructed during the Persian reign; two churches built in the period of Theodore, archbishop of Bozrah; the church of the Prophet Isaiah and the Church of Saint Menas, both built in 634 AD at the beginning of the Arab conquest.

Recently, other churches have come to light: the church of Saint Constantine (623 AD), the church of Saint John (619 AD) and the church of Saint George (691 AD), named after Archbishop George.

The abundance of Christian places of worship bear witness to the faith of the population and its love of Christ and the Virgin Mary.

Pella (Tabaqat-Fahl)

The original name of the city was Pehel Fahl: it is mentioned in ancient Egyptian writings dating from 1840 BC. After Alexander the Great's conquest (356–323 BC) Pehel fell under the domination of the Greeks and their culture. The change of name from Pehel to Pella dates from 310 BC, when a large number of families from Macedonia, to the north of Greece, settled here. It was these families who called the city Pella, after the capital of Macedonia, the birthplace of Alexander the Great.

Christianity spread to Pella at the beginning of the first century AD. The historian Eusebius (264–340 AD) records in his *History of the Church* that Vespasian, on being proclaimed emperor by the Roman legions, returned to Rome in 68 AD, entrusting his son Titus with the leadership of the war against Judea. The Christians, realising that the destruction of Jerusalem was imminent, left the city with their bishop, Simon, and settled in Pella and the surrounding region.

Pella was the birthplace, in the second century AD, of the famous writer Ariston, author of an apology of Christianity entitled *Debate between Jason and Papisco concerning Christ Our Lord*. It is an argument between a Jew and a Christian about whether Christ fulfilled the prophecies of the Old Testament.

The most important Christian remains are the West Church with its three naves, built in the fifth century AD; the East Church, and another church discovered behind the theatre. It should be remembered that Pella was a bishopric, and some of its bishops have gone down in history as eminent figures.

The city was destroyed and abandoned because of an earthquake in 746–747. Its ruins still await excavations which would do justice to its ancient glories.

Pella (Tabaqat Fahl). The impressive ruins of the city.

Rabbath Ammon (Amman)

Rabbath Ammon, the capital of the Ammonites, is often mentioned in the Bible. As with other Ammonite cities, here too the territorial borders were guarded by armed garrisons. The first Book of Samuel records that 'Nahash the Ammonite went up, and laid siege to Jabesh Gilead' (1 Samuel 11:1), imposing humiliating conditions on its inhabitants. The people of Jabesh urged the tribes of Israel to come to their aid. King Saul, furious at what was happening, gathered an army, split it into three divisions and launched a surprise attack on the enemy camp at dawn during the changing of the guard. Many Ammonites were slaughtered and the rest scattered, and Jabesh was saved.

The second Book of Samuel (cf. Chapters 10–11) records David's wars against the Ammonites: it was during one of these that he ordered Joab, the commander of his army, to arrange the death of Uriah the Hittite.

The Hebrews made no real attempt to capture Amman, because of the admonition in Deuteronomy 2:19:

> 'When you come near the land of the Ammonites, do not trouble them or wage war on them, for I will not give you possession of any land of the children of Ammon; I have given it to the descendents of Lot as a possession.'

We find prophecies of the destruction of Ammon in the Books of Amos (750 BC), Jeremiah (625 BC) and Zephaniah (c.630 BC).

As with Jerash and Gadara, the Romans took great care of Amman. They redesigned the city, demolishing many of the old houses and putting up new ones in their place, and building beautiful

Amman. Acropolis, with a glimpse of the city. In the foreground, the columns of the temple of Hercules.

streets. The great theatre, with its seating for 8,000 people, dates from 130 AD. The reign of Marcus Aurelius (161–180 AD) saw the building of the temple of Hercules on the hill of the citadel, the public baths, the market and the hippodrome. With the reconstruction of the old citadel and its towers, Amman became, in every aspect of its social life, a smaller version of Rome.

The churches which the Christians had built there were destroyed on the orders of the emperor Diocletian, who also decreed a bonfire of the Holy Scriptures in the central square. After the wave of persecutions died down, the Christians started rebuilding. Among the most significant religious buildings are two churches in the western part of the old city, a third beside the river, one on the citadel and another, in honour of Saint George, consecrated at the time of Polyeuctus, bishop of Amman.

After the battle of the Yarmuk, the Arabs dispersed and expelled the remnants of the Byzantine army, capturing Jerash, Tabaqat Fahl (Pella) and Beisan. Yazid bin Abi Sufyan then headed towards Amman, which he occupied on August 16th 636 AD. The Umayyads took care of the city, while the Abbasids neglected it, transferring their capital to Baghdad and condemning Amman to a period of serious architectural, commercial and cultural decline. Throughout the Middle Ages, until the end of the Ottoman Empire, Amman and the surrounding regions remained isolated from the rest of the world. The only interest the Turks showed in Jordan was in ensuring the safety of the roads used by the many pilgrims.

After the war between Turkey and Russia in 1877–1878, Russia conquered part of the Caucasus, forcing the local population to flee to the Ottoman Empire. Sultan Abd al-Hamid distributed them in regions where there was water. In 1878 a large number of Circassian families settled in the ruins of Amman, and more arrived in 1880.

Amman. The great theatre of the city, with seating for 8,000.

After the First World War, Emir Abdullah ibn Hussein settled in Amman, at a time when Transjordan was part of the British protectorate. When, in 1923, Great Britain officially recognised the emirate of Transjordan, it became a State under the leadership of the emir. In May 1946, with the end of the British mandate, Jordan became independent. The Parliament of Transjordan proclaimed Emir Abdullah king of the country, and the emirate of Transjordan became 'the Hashemite kingdom of Jordan'.

The martyrs of Amman

The Christians of Amman and its surroundings fell victim to the many persecutions which occurred in the empire during the first three centuries of the Christian era, especially the great persecution under Diocletian (284–305 AD), during which thousands of Christians were martyred. In February 303 AD the emperor ordered the destruction of all churches, a great bonfire of sacred texts, and the removal of all Christians from administrative or military posts.

The names of many of these martyrs have gone down in history, among them Elian, a seller of fabrics who had his shop near the northern gate of the city known as the 'gate of Jerash'; Theodosius and his companions; Cyril, Aquila, Damian, Rufus and Munthir, who were martyred in the great square on August 1st 304.

Worthy of mention is the detailed account of the martyrdom of a Roman officer, Zeno, and his companion Zena on June 23rd 304. Zeno was an officer of the legion stationed at Zizia. When he appeared before Philip, the governor of Amman, he openly declared his Christian identity. Imprisoned and wounded, he was visited by his servant and friend Zena, who had come to tend him. When the guards realised that the visitor was also a Christian, the governor arrested him and tried every way possible to persuade him to offer sacrifices to the pagan gods, but in vain. Both were tried in the open air in the lower city of Amman. Before dying, Zeno uttered the following prayer:

> 'O Lord Jesus, you have said: he who renounces himself, by me he will be saved. I have understood what you said and believe in your words.'

On March 21st, 2000, Pope John Paul II, celebrating mass in the stadium of Amman, remembered these martyrs:

> 'Today, as part of my jubilee pilgrimage, visiting some of the places linked to the mystery of salvation, Divine Providence has brought me to Jordan… Peter's successor is a pilgrim in this land blessed by the presence of Moses and Elijah, where Jesus himself taught and performed miracles (cf. Mark 10:1; John 10:40–42), and where the early Church bore witness through the lives of so many saints and martyrs. In this year of the Great Jubilee, the whole of the Church, and the Christian community of Jordan in particular, is spiritually united to me in a pilgrimage to the origins of our faith, a pilgrimage of conversion and repentance, reconciliation and peace.'

Zeno with his servant Zena. This painting of the two martyrs is preserved in the Latin Vicariate of Amman.

Sweifiyeh

Sweifiyeh may appear to the visitor to be a new town, a town without history, but its origins go back to ancient times. In 1970, the ruins of a church were

Sweifiyeh. Detail of the mosaic floor of the church.

discovered here, part of a monastery inhabited by monks who isolated themselves from the world and moved to the desert to find the tranquillity necessary to contemplate God. The name Sweifiyeh appears to derive from Sofia: wisdom.

The floor of the church was decorated with mosaics in the second half of the 6th century AD. The dedicatory inscription is badly damaged, but it is still possible to read the name of Bishop Thomas, who was the bishop of Amman at the time.

Khirbat al-Kursi

The ruins of Khirbat al-Kursi are situated one kilometre south of the hospital district of Amman.

They include an Ammonite tower, a church, a monastery, and two olive presses belonging to the monastery. There is also a mosque from the Umayyad period, which was re-used during the reign of the Mamelukes. Many inscriptions have

Khirbat al-Kursi. Ruins of the hill, west of Amman.

come to light, some in Greek, some in Syriac-Palestinian. The church appears to date from the middle of the sixth century AD.

Heshbon (Hesban)

This village, about nine kilometres north of Madaba, is the Heshbon mentioned in the Bible. The Romans changed its name to Hesbus. In the middle of the second millennium BC it was the capital of the kingdom of the Amorites, which extended from Madaba in the south to the kingdom of the Ammonites in the north and from the Dead Sea in the west to the desert in the east.

The Amorites' relationship with the surrounding kingdoms was sometimes peaceful, sometimes hostile. The Book of Numbers states that, at the time of Sihon king of Heshbon, the kingdom stretched as far as the valley of the river Arnon (Numbers 21:26). This was in about 1250 BC, the period when the Israelites were on their way to the Promised Land. According to Deuteronomy, when Moses approached the desert of Kedemoth, he sent envoys to Sihon, offering peace and asking permission to pass through the territory (cf. Deuteronomy

2:26–37). Sihon was suspicious, and not only rejected the request but rode out to confront the Israelites in battle at Jahaz. On that occasion, the Israelites defeated Sihon, seized his lands and cities and exterminated all the inhabitants.

According to the Book of Joshua (Joshua 13:15–21) and the Book of Numbers, Moses assigned Heshbon and all the cities of the plain to the tribe of Reuben. It became a border area between the tribe of Reuben and that of Gad (Joshua 13:26). Like three other cities of Jordan, Ramoth, Mahanaim and Jazer (Joshua 21:38–39), it was a city where involuntary homicides from the tribe of Gad could find refuge.

The region was invaded, first by the armies of Sargon II, king of Assyria (722–707 BC), which sent the population into exile, and in 597 by the Babylonian armies, led by Nebuchadnezzar, which occupied the region of Al Balqa. On both occasions, Heshbon was destroyed.

The prophets Isaiah (Isaiah 16:8) and Jeremiah (Jeremiah 48:2; 48:34; 49:3) lamented the fall of Heshbon. There is also a significant mention in the

Heshbon (Hesban). Remains of the church unearthed in the northern part of the excavations.

Song of Songs: written in about the sixth century BC, this poem refers to the city's two pools: 'Your eyes are like the pools of Heshbon, near the gate of Bath Rabbim.' (Song of Songs 7:4)

The most important Christian ruins so far brought to light are three churches and a large number of tombs from the Roman and Byzantine periods.

Madaba

Madaba is locate thirty kilometres south of Amman. Its fertile valley was the scene of constant struggle between the inhabitants of the region and the Israelites. The Book of Joshua (Joshua 13:16–23) records that the city was given to the tribe of Reuben.

Mesha, king of Moab, in the list of his victories over Israel, speaks of retaking Madaba (9th century BC). Isaiah also mentions the city, and prophesies its downfall (Isaiah 15:2–5).

The city was famous for the skill of its mosaic makers, who produced floors in Madaba, Nebo, Mukhayyat, Ma'in and Quweismeh. Some of these artists are known to posterity, as their names are inscribed on their mosaics. Among them are Na'um, Ciriaco and Thomas, who worked on the church in Mukhayyat; the monk Julian, who worked on the chapel of John in Mukhayyat; and Solomon, who worked on the church of the Apostles in Madaba.

More than ten churches containing wonderful mosaics have been unearthed. These mosaics give us a precious glimpse of daily life in the Byzantine period, with information about clothes, animals, birds, and environmental conditions, as well as a distillation of the religious and cultural thought of the region at that time.

Madaba. Mosaic in the so-called 'hall of Hippolytus'.

The most important mosaic is that known as the 'Madaba Mosaic Map', in the Greek Orthodox church, which is the oldest existing map of Jordan, Palestine and Egypt. Scholars believe that it was completed in about 565. The map was a gift or an ex-voto from the people of Madaba. Today, contemplating what remains of the map, it is possible to share the sentiments the Christian population of Madaba in the sixth century must have felt as they admired its holy places, its cities, mountains, valleys and pastures. With these mosaic pictures, the people of Madaba, then at the height of its glory, hoped to leave their children and posterity an image of their own love of Christ.

The name of Madaba is linked in Christian history to the council of Chalcedon (451 AD), which was attended by more than six hundred bishops, twenty of them Arabs. Among them was Caiano, bishop of Madaba, who was succeeded by Caiano II, disciple of the famous hermit Euthimius.

The Abarim mountains

In Deuteronomy 32:49 and 34:1–6 we read the
following:

> 'Go up into the Abarim mountains, to mount
> Nebo in the land of Moab, opposite Jericho, and
> behold the land of Canaan, which I am giving the
> children of Israel as a possession… And Moses
> went up from the plains of Moab to mount Nebo,
> to the top of Pisgah, opposite Jericho. And the
> Lord showed him the whole land… And Moses
> the servant of the Lord died there in the land of
> Moab, as the Lord had said. And He buried him
> in a valley in the land of Moab, opposite Beth
> Peor: but no man knows the place of his burial
> to this day.'

The Abarim mountains in Moab separate the Dead
Sea from the hills of Moab. The mountains were
given this name because most caravans moving
westwards from the eastern desert had to cross

Madaba. Detail of the
'Mosaic map' showing
the city of Jerusalem.

The Abarim mountains seen from the top.

them. Mount Nebo is one of these mountains and towers over Jericho and the land of Canaan.

When the Israelites arrived and camped on the Abarim mountains, the Moabite king, Balak son of Zippor, summoned Balaam and ordered him to curse the Israelites. God prevented this, and instead made Balaam bless them (Numbers 22–24).

According to an old tradition, Jeremiah, before the destruction of Jerusalem in 587 BC, managed to hide the ark of the covenant and the altar of incense in these mountains (2 Maccabees 2:4–7).

Mount Nebo (Siyagha)

Moses went up from the desert of Moab onto Mount Nebo, to the peak of Pisgah opposite Jericho, and there God showed him the Promised Land, saying:

> 'This is the land I promised Abraham, Isaac and Jacob, saying, I will give it to your descendants: I have let you see it with your eyes, but you will not enter it.' (Deuteronomy 34:4)

Aerial view of the whole area of excavations on Mount Nebo.

Moses died there and was buried in the valley, in the land of Moab, opposite Beth Peor. Deuteronomy 34:6 states that to this day nobody knows the whereabouts of his tomb.

Mount Nebo is situated to the west of Madaba, facing the mouth of the river Jordan and the city of Jericho. The mountain was also called 'Siyagha', a Syrian name meaning 'border', 'cell' or 'monastery', and which seems to refer both to the fact that Moses died without being able to cross the limit set for him by God and to the various monasteries which were built on the mountain over the centuries.

The Spanish pilgrim Egeria, who visited the holy places in 394 AD, mentions the memorial to Moses on Mount Nebo in her *Travel Diary*. According to her, many monks lived there, including some who sheltered travellers. On the summit of the mountain she discovered a small chapel and two monuments, one on either side. Later pilgrims tried hard to find these monuments. It took research, excavations and scientific studies to solve the mystery. Eventually, a church with three apses dating from the fourth century was brought to light. The present altar was built over existing tombs and mosaics. On both sides are the remains of two small mortuary chapels. In the northern part, a baptismal font was added, while the southern part was decorated with a large cross. The baptistry was also covered with mosaics, the work of three artists, Soel, Syam and Elia, who 'signed' it in August 531.

The new church, with its three naves, was built in 597 during the time of Sergius, bishop of Madaba. In 608, a small chapel was added in honour of the 'Virgin Mary, Mother of God'. In it was found this inscription:

> 'O Christ our God, marvellous Creator of all things, work on the church of the Mother of God was completed thanks to the holy bishop Leontius, with the help of two priests and abbots, Martirius and Theodore.'

Mount Nebo. Mosaic floor in the diakonicon-baptistry of the great 'Moses memorial'.

This complex bears witness to the continuing significance to Christians of the prophet Moses, who is described in these words in the Book of Sirach: 'Moses who was loved by God and by men, and whose memory is blessed…' (Sirach 45:1).

Pope John Paul II contemplates the Holy Land from Mount Nebo, during his pilgrimage to the Holy Land (March 20th 2000).

The shrine, the church and the monasteries were subject to all the political and military changes which left their mark on the country, as well as major earthquakes in 551, 1016 and 1033 AD.

On March 20th 2000, in the central nave of the main church, Pope John Paul II knelt in silent prayer, and in a spirit of reverence and piety. Then he spoke these words:

'Now I have reached the heights of Mount Nebo, where Moses, before his death, contemplated the Promised Land without being able to enter it. In this culmination of the Exodus, we glimpse an image of the life of the Church and of all mankind, waiting for the fulfilment of God's final promise… Let us raise our prayer to God Almighty for all the people of the Promised Land: Jews, Muslims and Christians… Spread to all those who live here the gift of true peace, justice and brotherhood.'

The city of Nebo (Mukhayyat)

The ruins of Mukhayyat are located four kilometres
south-east of Mount Nebo. They are the remains
of the ancient city of Nebo. Their location is
spectacular, surrounded as they are by valleys on all
sides. The history of the city is linked to that of three
other cities in Jordan: Ramoth, Mahanaim and Jazer
(Joshua 21:38–39). The earliest traces date from the
thirteenth century BC.

The Book of Numbers (33:47) records that the
children of Israel, leaving Almon Diblathaim,
camped on the mountains of Abarim near the city
of Nebo, which the children of Reuben had rebuilt
(Numbers 32:38). In the ninth century BC, Mesha,
king of Dibon and Moab, laid siege to the city,
defeating the Israelites and destroying their altars.

Khirbat al-Mukhayyat.
Mosaic floor in the
church of Saints Lot
and Procopius.

From that point, it was a Moabite city, as recorded in Isaiah 15:2–3 and Jeremiah 48:1–2.

The ruins which can be seen by the visitor include churches, houses, tombs, and presses for wine and oil. From the middle of the fourth century, Nebo was a flourishing Christian town. Christianity, in fact, spread widely throughout the region, once the persecutions had stopped: the Christian communities began to build churches as a sign of their faith and piety.

The oldest church in Mukhayyat (Nebo) is the church of Saints Amos and Casiseos, which dates from the fourth century, that is, immediately after the persecutions. It is situated in the southern part of the valley of Afarit, where the village now stands. The people of the village used many of its stones to build their houses.

Baal Meon (Main). The springs of Zarqa Ma'in.

Next to the church there was a monastery, the chapel of which was called the 'chapel of the priest John'. It was decorated with mosaics, the work of the monk Julian. John, from whom the chapel takes its name, was the benefactor who financed its construction.

In the upper part of the city is the church of Saint George, and, opposite it, a small monastery. The church dates from the middle of the sixth century AD.

To the north of the citadel is the church of Saints Lot and Procopius. Procopius was martyred in Cesarea in 303 AD. He was originally from Jerusalem and had a large following in the area.

Baal Meon (Ma'in)

Ma'in, a Biblical city, is recorded in Numbers (Numbers 32:38) and Joshua (Joshua 13:17). It is mentioned in the stele commemorating the victory of Mesha, king of Moab, in the ninth century BC:

'I am Mesha, son of Kemosh, king of Moab
the Dibonite. I built Baal Meon and dug its
reservoir.'

Baal Meon means 'god of water', an etymology
preserved in its present name: Ma'in. The reservoir
mentioned still exists and can be found among the
ruins to the south of the village. It was, and still is,
the last inhabited place on the road that leads to
the hot springs at Zarqa Ma'in.

In the north wing of the western church an
inscription has been found, which states that
there was a hostel near the springs.

In the Roman period, the historian Eusebius
of Caesarea (265–340 AD) writes:

'Baal Meon, beyond the Jordan, is a large
village near the mountain with the thermal
waters, in the land of Arabia, and is situated
at the ninth milestone south of Hesbus
(Hesban).'

Among the principal Christian ruins, the church
of the Acropolis, on the top of the hill, is worthy
of note. An inscription in the ruins suggests that
the mosaic which can be seen there dates from
719–720 AD, that is, during the Umayyad period.
In the central nave there is a strip of mosaic
depicting geographical locations. Ten can still be
seen, among them Karak, Rabbath, Gadara
(Umm Qais), Gadara (near Salt) and Hesban.

Another Christian building is the church on the
western slope of the hill. It consists of three naves
and two rows of columns. Finally, mention should
be made of the monastic complex situated on an
isolated height south of the village, comprising a
chapel, the monks' cells, a well, some caves, a
storehouse and the remains of a wall.

Machaerus (Mukawir)

Situated thirty kilometres south of Madaba, the
fortress of Machaerus was built by Alexander
Jannaeus – a Hasmonean, descended from the
Maccabees – in 90 BC as a stronghold against
Nabataean invaders. Destroyed by the Romans in
57 BC, it was rebuilt by Herod the Great as a fortress
and palace, a place for amusements and baths.

The fortress of
Machaerus at dawn.

According to the historian Flavius Josephus,
it was here that John the Baptist was imprisoned.
The story of his martyrdom is told in Mark 6:14–29:
Herod Antipas, son of Herod the Great, had
divorced his wife to marry his brother's wife,
Herodias, while his brother was still alive. John the
Baptist openly denounced this act, and in so doing
incurred the hatred of Herodias.

Herod celebrated his birthday with a banquet
for the nobles and commanders of Galileee, at which
Herodias' daughter Salome danced. Herod was so
impressed that he promised to give her whatever

Machaerus, seen from
the east, at sunrise. In
the background, the
Dead Sea.

Machaerus. Aerial view of the excavations of Herod's fortress.

she asked, even half the kingdom. Spurred on by her mother, the young woman asked for the head of John the Baptist.

Herod's fortress was destroyed by Titus, the son of the emperor Vespasian and himself a future emperor, in 71 AD. Nobody tried to rebuild it, but the village which Herod had built on the eastern height remained inhabited until the end of the Byzantine period. It was called Machaerus, hence the Arab name Mukawir.

It is worth recalling that the fortress of Machaerus contains the oldest existing mosaic in Jordan. It dates from the end of the first century BC, at the time of the rebuilding of the fortress.

Dibon (Dhiban)

Dhiban is a town situated about thirty kilometres south of Madaba, on the road between Madaba and Karak.

When the Hebrews, coming from Sinai, reached the border of Heshbon, they fought its army, defeated it and captured the city. Dhiban and other towns in the area suffered the same fate. The city was given to Reuben, as recorded in Joshua 13:16–17 and Numbers 21:31.

Dhiban. The present-day village with a glimpse of the ancient walls.

In 1868 the inhabitants of the village found the famous stele of Mesha, king of Moab in the ninth century BC, with its inscription beginning with these words: 'I am Mesha, son of Kemosh, king of Moab, the Dibonite.'

The city is also mentioned in Jeremiah 48:21–22 and in the *Onomasticon* of Eusebius of Caesarea, dating from the first half of the fourth century, where Dhiban is described as a 'broad city near the river Arnon (Wadi Mujib)'.

Mesha's stele, discovered at Dhiban in 1868.

Mephaath (Umm ar-Rasas)

The ruins of Umm ar-Rasas are situated thirty kilometres south-east of Madaba. In July 1986, the department of archaeology began excavations on the site, north of the ruins, where today we find a complex including the church of Saint Stephen. Inscriptions discovered inside the church confirm the ancient name of the city: Mephaath. It is mentioned in the Book of Joshua:

> 'And Moses had given an inheritance to the tribe of Reuben, to each of their families; and their territory was from Aroer, on the bank of the river Arnon… Heshbon, and all the cities on the plateau: Dibon, Bamoth Baal, Beth Baal Meon, Jahaz, and Kedemoth, Mephaath…' (Joshua 13:15 et seq.)

The same places are mentioned in Jeremiah 48:21.

Eusebius of Caesarea states, in his geographical work the *Onomasticon*, that a unit of the Roman army was stationed in Mephaath, on the edges of the desert, in the fourth century.

In the eleventh century Al-Bakri made Mephaath a village in the region of greater Syria called Balqa.

Among the principal ruins in Umm ar-Rasas are the remains of a Roman military camp, a rectangular fort surrounded by solid walls and supported by numerous towers and buttresses. It had entrances to the east, north and south, joined among themselves by streets that crossed the whole camp. The area to the north of the camp is probably the site of the ancient city, which already existed before the Romans arrived. There have been finds in this area dating from the Nabataean, Roman and Byzantine periods. About one kilometre north of the military camp is a watchtower fifteen metres high, surrounded by a square in which there was once a church.

The excavations at Umm ar-Rasas are not yet complete, and it is difficult to determine with any accuracy the number of churches in the area.

Mephaath (Umm ar-Rasas). Part of the ruins of the city.

KACTP
MEΦ

Mephaath (Umm ar-Rasas). Detail of the mosaic found in the 'Church of the Lions'.

So far, fourteen have been found, four inside the perimeter of the camp, and ten outside. Most date from the sixth and seventh centuries. Among them, the church of Saint Stephen, built on a basilica plan, is worthy of note. The building itself is plain, but it has a mosaic floor rich in figurations, which makes it, along with the map in Madaba, a work of art unique among the ruins of Jordan. In the long narrow space between the columns the artists have depicted a number of cities in Palestine, Jordan and Egypt. Among the cities of Jordan we find: Mephaath, Philadelphia/Amman, Madaba, Heshbon/Hesban,

Baal Meon/Ma'in, Areopolis/Rabba, Karak-
Moba/Karak, Diblathon and Limbon, which is
probably still buried under the ruins of the city
of Libb.

Arnon (Wadi Mujib)

Four kilometres south of Dhiban can be found a
deep canyon between two mountain ranges: these
are the high bare mountains and deep valley crossed
by the river Mujib. The scene is a unique one, and
makes a great impression on visitors. As one
descends into the canyon down the narrow, winding
road, the scarcity of water is very striking.

The valley has an ancient name, Arnon, which
is often mentioned in the Bible. The mountains to
the north and south of the valley belonged to the
kingdom of the Moabites. The Bible records that
the king of the Amorites did battle with the king of
Moab and conquered all the land as far as the Arnon
(cf. Numbers 21:26). Other Biblical references can
be found in Deuteronomy 2:24; 3:8; 4:48; Joshua
12:1; 13:9; Judges 11:13; Isaiah 16:2 and Jeremiah
48:20.

Arnon. Mouth of the river, with part of the deep canyon caused by erosion.

Rabbath Moab (Rabba)

The town of Rabba is situated twelve kilometres
north of Karak. Its ancient name was Rabbath
Moab, which the Greeks changed to Areopolis.
Many of its ruins are still buried underground
and beneath the houses, but the few which can be
glimpsed are an eloquent testimony to its former
splendour. The remains of the Roman-era temple
are worth a visit.

Eusebius of Caesarea (265–340 AD) mentions a
major earthquake which struck the city in his time.

Rabba is famous for its resistance to Christianity,
which continued even when the religion could be
freely practised. The historian Sozomeneus of Gaza,
who lived in the fourth century AD, records in his
History of the Church how the Emperor Theodosius
I (347–395 AD) had to issue a decree against the
families of Rabba to overcome their opposition to
Christianity. Nevertheless, by the beginning of the
fifth century, the city was entirely Christian. Among

Rabba (Rabboth
Moab). Remains of the
Roman-era temple.

Rabba (Rabboth Moab). Architrave of one of the churches discovered in the area. A similar architrave has been found at Umm ar-Rasas.

its bishops were Anastasius, who took part in the council of Ephesus (499 AD), Policarpus who participated in the council of Jerusalem (518 AD) and Bishop Elias.

Many inscriptions have been found, which have made it possible to reconstruct the history of Rabba. One of them, found in a church, states that the building was renovated in 492 after an earthquake, when a certain John was bishop. Another inscription, referring to 'our father, Saint Stephen, archbishop', dates from 689 AD, during the Umayyad period, in the reign of the caliph Abd al-Malik bin Marwan (685–705 AD), from which it can be inferred that the city was an archbishopric at the time of the Umayyads. Another inscription bears a prayer testifying to the devotion of Rabba's citizens to the Virgin Mary: 'O Mother of God, help your servants!'

Kir-Haraseth (Karak)

The town of Karak is situated about 120 kilometres south of Amman.

It is mentioned in the third chapter of 2 Kings: after the death of Ahab, king of Israel, the king of Moab decided to rebel against Israel. The king of Israel and the king of Judah formed an alliance

against him, crossed the desert of Edom with their armies, entered the cities of the Moabites and destroyed everything in their path. When they reached Kir-haraseth (Karak), they surrounded the city. Seeing that the battle was going against him, the king of Moab took his firstborn son, the heir to the throne, and offered him as a burnt offering on the walls of the city. Paradoxically, this extreme act forced the kings of Israel and Judah to retreat, and they returned defeated to their own lands. This event took place when Joram was king of Israel (852–841 BC).

Karak is also mentioned in Isaiah 16:11 and Jeremiah 48:36. In 646 BC, Assurbanipal, king of Assyria (668–626 BC), conquered Moab, destroyed its cities and killed a large number of its inhabitants. Karak was one of these cities.

Karak. Remains of the Crusader castle.

Ader

The history of the city of Ader, seven kilometres east of Karak, is closely connected with that of Karak and its surroundings.

Its ruins date from thousands of years ago and
are still buried underground, beneath the houses
and streets, and may be irreparably damaged. The
word Ader in Syriac means 'farm' or 'threshing
floor'.

Many archaeologists have visited the area, trying
to reconstruct its history from the evidence of the
surface ruins (houses, walls, buildings, the remains of
churches). According to Albright, the city dates back
to the last part of the first Bronze Age: it had a period
of great prosperity between 2200 and 1800 BC.

Ader. Menir (Sarbut).
Prehistoric obelisk.

Ader. Cross carved in the rock, first half of the third century AD. The cave housing it can be found inside the Latin parochial complex.

A temple was built in the northern part of the city in about the year 2000 BC, the remains of which could still be seen in 1924. Unfortunately, local families then used its stones to build houses. In the area to the north east of the temple are three sacred stones (dolmens), of which only one has remained standing.

Albright's explorations have demonstrated that the lower part of what remains of the walls of the city date from the Moabite period, that is, the ninth century BC, the central part to the Nabataean period, and the upper part to the Roman period.

Most of the Byzantine remains, including the fortifications and the churches, suffered the same fate as the temple: their stones ended up as part of the houses.

In the 1930s, the archaeologist Regina Canova found a number of tombs, carved with crosses and inscriptions, from the Byzantine period. They bear sentences such as: 'Here lies Anastasia, daughter of Archelaus, 56 years old' and 'Here lies John, son of Sophonia, 6 years old'. Among the best preserved Christian remains are the crosses found on the walls of the cave beneath the Latin parish: they date from the first part of the third century AD and are an excellent testimony to the faith of the first generations of Christians, who suffered the same persecutions as their brothers in the region and the empire. But even this testimony was nearly wiped out: unaware of their value, a woman, who may have wanted to clean the walls of the cave, tried to erase the crosses, and some were lost.

Legio (Lejjun)

Lejjun was a Roman military camp, the ruins of which bear witness to the Romans' concern with defending the borders of the desert from the incursions of the Arab tribes who tried to expel the Romans and gain control of the area.

The camp was 242 metres long and 190 wide, and was surrounded by walls which were as much as two and a half metres thick. At the four corners were circular towers, each with its own door, and between them various defensive emplacements. The camp was crossed by two streets: the main one went from north to south, while a street from the eastern door met it in the centre of the camp, where the general headquarters was situated.

The main gate was the eastern one. On either side were the barracks of the soldiers and officers. Each room could contain eight people. The officers' rooms were larger than those of the soldiers.

It would appear that, from the end of the fourth century AD, the soldiers, given the diminishing threat from the nearby tribes, took up trade and agriculture.

Legio. Remains of the Roman camp.

Of equal significance are the remains of a Byzantine church dating from the fifth century. Plain in style, it was used until the middle of the sixth century, when the camp was evacuated because of the earthquake of 551 AD.

When, towards the middle of the sixth century, the Roman Empire began to relax its defensive policy towards the 'Arab border', fear and insecurity among the local population led to increasing emigration.

Petra

Originally an Edomite city, it was only later that Petra became a Nabataean city.

The Nabataeans were skilled traders, and they facilitated exchanges between India and the Far East, Egypt, Syria, Greece and Rome, making the city an important trading centre and a meeting point for many different cultures.

The Nabataeans have gone down in history for their buildings, temples and tombs, carved with extreme refinement out of the sandstone rock. The diverse colours of the rock increase the beauty of the buildings. A poet wrote:

'Born out of the rock, Petra grew as if by magic: eternal, humble, fascinating and unique.'

Petra. Staircase leading to a Nabataean tomb in the little Siq. (Al Baydha).

Petra. View of the Khasnet from inside the Siq.

Among the 'arts' of the Nabataeans, their skill in storing water should not be forgotten: they built a network of dams, canals and reservoirs.

The Romans occupied Petra in 105 AD, and called the land of the Nabataeans 'Province of Arabia', with Bostra in Syria as its capital. When the Romans divided Palestine and Jordan into 'first', 'second' and 'third Palestine', Petra, already Christian, became the seat of the archbishop of third Palestine. The city was destroyed in the earthquake of 746–748 AD.

Among the most important archaeological remains are:

The *Siq*. The only passage leading into the city is a gorge between the rocks, 1200 metres long, where a multitude of colours intersect and overlap. The Nabataeans dug a canal in the rock, on the left-hand side, to carry the water from the springs of Wadi Musa to the city. There are numerous niches in the rock walls, in which the Nabataeans placed statues of their gods, including Dhushara.

'Pharaoh's Treasury.' It is both a temple and a tomb, and was given this name because of the belief that Pharaoh had hidden his treasure in the urn in the upper part of the structure. It dates from the time of the Nabataean king Al-Harith III (84–56 BC).

A *Roman amphitheatre* and a group of tombs carved in the rock.

The *Qasr al-Bint*, a temple built by the Nabataeans in the first century BC in honour of Allat.

A *monastery*, which was originally a pagan temple and was then transformed by the Christians into a place of worship (as they also did with certain tombs).

An *altar*, between 'Pharaoh's treasury' and the Roman amphitheatre.

A *large church*, discovered a few years ago.

Lot's Cave (Ain Abata)

Lot was the son of Abraham's brother Harran. He accompanied his uncle Abraham on his journey from the land of Mesopotamia to the land of Canaan. Like him, he owned sheep, cattle and tents. One day a quarrel broke out between his herdsmen and those of Abraham. 'And Abraham said to Lot, Let there be no quarrelling, between you and me, or between your herdsmen and my herdsmen, for we are brothers.' He then asked his nephew to choose the land he wanted. Lot chose the whole valley of

Dead Sea. Salt formations.

the Jordan. They separated, and Abraham settled in the land of Canaan while Lot travelled east to the cities of the valley, pitching his tents near Sodom (cf. Genesis 13:8–13).

Soon after, Sodom and Gomorrah was attacked and captured by four kings. Lot was carried off with his possessions. Abraham, informed of what had happened by a survivor, gathered a group of men and pursued the enemy as far as Dan. There, he attacked them by night and defeated them (cf. Genesis 14:8–16).

Sodom and Gomorrah return to centre stage in Chapter 19 of Genesis, which tells how the cities were destroyed, how Lot and his wife were saved, and how Lot's wife, worried by the loss of her possessions, turned around and was transformed into a pillar of salt. Jesus refers to this story in Luke 17:32. After the destruction of Sodom and Gomorrah, Lot moved to Zoar, and settled in this hilly area with his daughters.

These episodes, set in Jordan, in the area around the Dead Sea, led Christians to revere Lot for his piety. While it may be difficult today to find a

Christian with a high regard for Lot, many imaginative believers over the centuries have searched for the pillar of salt into which Lot's wife was immortalised. There are stunning natural landscapes on the eastern side of the road which runs parallel to the Dead Sea, and many people, remembering the story of Lot's wife, have seen in them something resembling a statue or a pillar of salt.

Lot's Cave, which has become a destination for pilgrimage, was built by monks and other Christians in the first centuries AD in a place known today as Ain Abata, at the foot of one of the mountains of Ghor as-Safi, in the southern part of the Dead Sea. There were many monks living an isolated life of prayer and worship in these deserted areas. Tens of thousands of Christians came here to receive the blessings of Saint Lot. Excavations in the area have unearthed the remains of a rectangular building, eighteen metres long and seven wide. It was built on the edge of a sheer cliff and reinforced by two supporting walls. Inside the remains of seven arches have been found, parts of a large reservoir intended to collect water for irrigation. For personal use, though, the monks drew water from a stream

Aerial view of the shrine dedicated to Saint Lot, Ain Abata.

located on the side of the mountain, to the north-west.

In 1991, a large church was found near the cave, and was identified as the place where Lot sheltered from the destruction of Sodom and Gomorrah. In one of its three naves a mosaic was discovered, with a four-line inscription referring to Bishop Jacobus and the abbot of the monastery, Sozomeneus. The inscription dates from 606 AD, which is the period in which the church was decorated with mosaics. The sacred buildings in honour of Saint Lot can also be dated to the same period.

Shobak

Shobak Castle, built by Baldwin I in 1115 AD, during the Crusades, is situated on the top of a hill north-east of the village of Shobak. There are two churches in the castle, one of which is visible as we climb the stairs to the north of the castle entrance.

Shobak. View of the Crusader castle.

Wadi Rum

Wadi Rum is situated twenty-five kilometres north of Aqaba. It is an ideal place to experience the romantic charm of the desert, its natural beauty, its sandstone mountains. It seems like a lunar landscape.

Anyone wishing to enjoy a spectacular view of the valley and its mountains should walk along the Wadi, climb one of its mountains and savour the silence and majesty of nature.

When the inhabitants of Edom and Moab refused to allow the Israelites to cross their lands, the latter were forced to enter the eastern desert, taking the roads that pass through Wadi Rum. From here the Israelites moved north, towards Kademoth (cf. Numbers 21:4).

Wadi Rum. A glimpse of the typical landscape.

Ezion Geber (Tell al-Khaleifeh)

Tell al-Khaleifeh is situated west of Aqaba, close to the border between Israel and Jordan. Here we can see what are almost certainly the ruins of Ezion Geber. The first Book of Kings states:

> 'And King Solomon built a fleet of ships in Ezion Geber, which is near Elath, on the shore of the Red Sea, in the land of Edom. And Hiram sent servants, sailors who had knowledge of the sea, to serve in the fleet with the servants of Solomon. They sailed to the land of Ophir, and brought back gold... which they delivered to King Solomon.' (1 Kings 9:26–28)

In 1998 parts of the walls of the Nabataean-Roman city and the remains of a rectangular church were discovered, whose walls had been built out of mud. The church is twenty-six metres long and sixteen wide. Bronze coins and fragments of vases have been found during excavations, making it possible to date the church as far back as the third century AD, which makes it the oldest church to have been discovered in Jordan.

Tell al-Khaleifeh. Ruins of the ancient city.

The River Jordan. Early Christian accounts locate the baptism of Jesus at the eighth mile north of the shore of the Dead Sea.

The river Jordan

The river Jordan marks the border both between Jordan and Israel and between Jordan and Palestine. It is mentioned many times in the Old and New Testaments. From a Biblical point of view, it is one of the most sacred places of all, and is of great symbolic significance. Christ sanctified it with his baptism, many Old Testament prophets crossed it, and the apostles and saints themselves considered it very important.

The Dead Sea

The river Jordan flows into the Dead Sea, which is an enclosed basin, with no outlets. It stretches for seventy-five kilometres, and its width varies from six to sixteen kilometres. Because of its high salt and mineral content, the Dead Sea is completely lacking in vegetable or animal life. It is the lowest point on the surface of the earth, being about 400 metres below sea level.

Sunset over
the Dead Sea.

In the Bible it is called both 'salt sea' and 'eastern sea' (Deuteronomy 3:17; Joshua 3:16: Ezekiel 47:18). Currently it forms the border between Jordan and Israel and between Jordan and Palestine.

Bethany beyond the Jordan

The region of Bethany beyond the Jordan was the centre of John the Baptist's activities, and the place where Jesus began his public life.

Map showing the finds in the area of excavation: Elijah's hill and the site of Jesus' baptism.

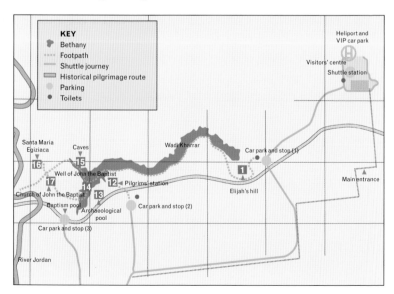

Bethany is still buried underground and its real position remains unknown. Perhaps it can be found among the ruins about two hundred metres west of Elijah's hill, a place where no excavations have yet been carried out. This area is known as Wadi Kharrar in reference to the murmur of the waters in the valley.

It was in Bethany that John, seeing Jesus approaching, said: 'Behold the Lamb of God who takes away the sins of the world.' It was here, too, that Jesus met some of his disciples (cf. John 1:35–51). In Chapter 19 of his gospel, Matthew writes:

> 'Jesus… left Galilee, and went into the territory of Judea, on the other side of the Jordan; large crowds followed him; and he healed them there.'

When Jesus went up to Jerusalem, he avoided Samaria, by crossing the Jordan, and re-entering near Jericho. While he was in Transjordan, some Pharisees approached him, and tried to trap him: 'Is it lawful for a man to divorce his wife for whatever reason he wishes?' (cf. Matthew 19:3; Mark 10:2). Some children were also brought to him, so that he could put his hands on them and bless them (cf. Matthew 19:13–15).

During the Feast of Dedication, Jesus revealed his true identity to the Jews. They responded by trying to stone him, but he escaped to Bethany:

> 'Jesus went back again across the Jordan to the place where John had been baptising, and there he stayed.' (John 10:40)

John continues: 'And many came to him… and many believed in him there' (John 10:41–42). It is not difficult to imagine the scene: the inhabitants of the surrounding towns, Gadara (El-Gadur near Salt),

Madaba, Hesban, Dhiban, Mephaath and Amman, presenting themselves to Jesus, in order to hear him and follow him. Jesus had many friends in Bethany.

The excavations at Wadi Kharrar bring us face to face with the oldest Christian traditions, which have long been forgotten. They recall many wonderful episodes in both the Old and New Testaments, but to fully grasp their significance we must keep our Bibles open before us.

Site of Jesus' baptism. Aerial view of the three churches discovered by archaeologists.

The Baptism Site

Some 1,800 metres from Elijah's hill runs the river Jordan: it is here that Christians recall the baptism of Jesus. The place is generally known as the 'Baptism Site'. Matthew (3:5–6 and 16) states that Christ was baptised by John in the Jordan. Mark writes: 'At that time Jesus came from Nazareth in Galilee, and was baptised by John in the Jordan' (Mark 1:9). As he was emerging from the water, he saw the skies open, and the Holy Spirit descended on him in the form of

Station for pilgrims between the baptism site and 'Elijah's hill'. Byzantine remains.

a dove. A voice from heaven declared: 'You are my beloved son, and I am well pleased with you.' (Mark 1:11)

Since the earliest days, Christians have wondered where exactly Jesus was baptised. Obviously, it is impossible to pinpoint the exact location. But, on the basis of the information contained in the Bible, it has been deduced that John baptised Christ at the point where the Jordan is crossed by the Roman road which joins the cities of Jericho and Jerusalem with the cities to the east of the river: Livias, Heshbon, Madaba and Ammon.

Not only is John believed to have baptised in this area, but it is also here that the Israelites, led by Joshua son of Nun, are supposed to have crossed the river on the way to Jericho.

Recent excavations in this area have demonstrated that, once the persecutions were over, the Christians built churches and monasteries on the eastern bank of the river to keep alive the memory of Jesus' baptism.

At present, three churches can be seen, about 100 metres east of the river, and one kilometre from Elijah's hill. A first church was built on the bank of the river, but was damaged by floods. Towards the end of the fifth century AD, the emperor Anastasius I (491–518) built another church over it, raised up on arches to protect it from the floods. From the new church, a staircase led down to the river, allowing the pilgrims to bathe or to collect a little water to take to their own countries as a relic. A huge column with a cross at the top was placed in the middle of the river. Later the emperor Justinian (527–565 AD) showed his fondness for the sacred building by restoring it.

Site of Jesus' baptism. Ruins of three churches unearthed by excavations. In the fifth century, the emperor Anastasius had the church of the Baptism of Jesus built on the eastern bank of the Jordan and the monastery of Safsafas, with the chapel of Saint John, on Elijah's hill.

It is worth recalling that on the mosaic map in Madaba, which gives us a 'snapshot' of the region in the sixth century AD, Bethany beyond the Jordan, the place of Jesus' baptism, and the Elijah's hill appear as distinct places.

One question remains unresolved: at that time, were these churches on the bank of the river?

Because of earthquakes or landslides, the course of the Jordan, has often, in fact, changed, as is proved by the most recent change, registered during the earthquake of 1927.

Elijah's Hill

The most important episode in the life of the prophet Elijah was his ascent to heaven in a whirlwind. The second Book of Kings (2:8–11) records that Elijah, having stopped with Elisha on the banks of the Jordan, took his cloak, rolled it, and with it struck the waters, which parted so that the two could cross over on dry land. The power of God was working in him up until the last moment. The Bible does not precisely say that he went up to heaven in a chariot of fire, but that 'he went up in a whirlwind' (2 Kings 2:11), in other words that he returned to his Lord, like every righteous man who enters heaven.

Elijah's hill. General view.

Elijah's hill. Ruins of the church.

The text gives a clear idea of how Elijah died. Most probably, he withdrew into the desert, as he had often done at other times, and never returned. Popular tradition then gave to rise fantastic interpretations, inferring things from the text which the text does not say and explaining the words of the Scriptures as if Elijah had risen to heaven body and soul. Hence also the tradition relating to his return, in visible form, on the 'day of the Lord'.

After the period of persecutions, the Christians built a monastery in memory of Elijah's ascent to heaven, on the hill of Tell Kharrar, to the west of the Kharrar springs. Recent excavations carried out on

Elijah's hill. Third-fourth century baths, used for the baptism and immersion of pilgrims.

Elijah's hill.
Inscription discovered
on the floor of the
church inside the
monastery. It mentions
the Igumen Retorius,
of the fifth-sixth
centuries.

the hill, which is also known as 'Elijah's hill', have
unearthed the remains of a church, pools, a canal
which carried the water from a spring to the
Wadi Kafrain, a well, a cistern, and the remains
of a monastery dating from the fifth and sixth
centuries AD.

An unknown historian, in his life of Saint Helena,
mother of the emperor Constantine, records that
Helena went to the Jordan, crossed it at the point at
which tradition placed the baptism site, and visited
the cave where John the Baptist had dwelt. She
herself ordered a church to be built, and visited the
hill where 'Elijah's ascent to heaven' was supposed
to have taken place.

Another pilgrim, from the city of Bordeaux
in France (333 AD) refers to having visited 'the
hill from which Elijah ascended to heaven in a
whirlwind', as does the pilgrim Theodosius (350 AD),
who tells of his visit to the place where Christ was
baptised: he states that there is also water beyond
the river, and that the place of Jesus' baptism is the
hill Harmoun, a place which recalls Elijah's ascent
to heaven in a chariot of fire. Among other things,
he adds that the valley is peopled by monks and
hermits. The same place was also visited by many

pilgrims during the sixth and seventh centuries AD.
Among those worthy of mention are an anonymous
pilgrim from Piacenza (570 AD), Arculfo (670 AD)
and Wilbrand (720–27 AD).

Elijah's hill. Monks' caves.

The abbot Daniel, a Russian monk of the twelfth
century (1106–1107 AD), writes:

> 'On the eastern side of the river Jordan, near the
> place where Christ was baptised, is Elijah's hill,
> where he was carried to heaven in a chariot of
> fire.'

The name 'Elijah's hill' also recurs on a Turkish
map from the First World War: a tradition probably
inherited from Jewish beliefs.

The prophet Elijah
and John the Baptist

It should be clear to us from their work that the holy
writers responsible for the text of the Bible had a
sense of 'history' which is simultaneously human

and divine. Their 'history' takes place in time, but its roots are deep in eternity.

This needs to be borne in mind whenever we read and meditate on the Holy Scriptures.

The unity of the messages of Elijah and John the Baptist is obvious. St John's Gospel states clearly that Bethany beyond Jordan, near the place of Christ's baptism, was the Baptist's centre of activity:

> 'All these things happened in Bethany beyond the Jordan, where John was baptising.'
> (John 1:28)

This is an important region from a Biblical point of view, and is referred to in the prophetic texts. We have only to think of the prophet Malachi, who writes:

> 'Behold, I will send you the prophet Elijah… and he will turn the hearts of the fathers to their children, and the hearts of the children to their fathers.' (Malachi 4:5–6)

After his transfiguration, Jesus spoke on this subject to his apostles:

Elijah's hill. Prayer hall, dating from the sixth century, south west of the source of the Wadi Karrar.

> 'Elijah has already come, and they did not recognise him, but did to him whatever they wished.' (Matthew 17:12)

This Elijah, in fact, appeared in the same region from which the first Elijah had left. And his preaching is that prophesied by Malachi and repeated by Luke in his gospel:

> 'To turn the hearts of the fathers to their children, and the disobedient to the wisdom of the just; to make ready a people prepared for the Lord.' (Luke 1:17)

Mount Nebo towers over all these places. After the death of Moses, God said to Joshua:

> 'Arise now, you and all these people, and cross the river Jordan, into the land which I am giving them, the children of Israel.' (Joshua 1:2)

It was from here that the Israelites entered the Promised Land. This was also the road along which the exiles returned from Babylon (Ezra 1:1–6). John the Baptist, with his constant call to conversion, reminded the people of all these events from the Old Testament, and prepared them for the coming of the Lord. It is certainly not without significance that Jesus began his public ministry after being baptised in the Jordan by John, the 'witness' of Moses and Elijah. In the light of this continuity, he set off to establish the new covenant through his own death and resurrection.

Jesus and Peter

According to St John's Gospel, Jesus met five of his first disciples at Bethany beyond the Jordan (John 1:37–51). The first was Andrew, who brought his

Ruins of the church situated south of Elijah's hill. It was beneath this arch that Pope John Paul II prayed with the Christian people of Jordan. The place is now known as the 'church of John Paul II'.

brother Simon to him. On seeing Simon, Jesus looked at him and said:

> 'You are Simon, the son of John, but you will
> be called Cephas, which means Peter: a rock.'

From that first moment, Jesus' gaze made a deep impression on Peter.

According to Matthew, Simon was already called Peter before the Twelve were chosen (Matthew 10:2). Jesus would again use this name when Simon demonstrated his own faith in him by recognising him as the Son of God (Matthew 16:16–18).

According to Mark and Luke, on the other hand, Jesus did not give Simon the name Peter when he chose the twelve Apostles (Mark 3:16; Luke 6:14).

This should come as no surprise: Jesus uses the name Cephas-Peter above all at important moments, such as the choice of the Twelve and the profession of faith in Christ Son of God.

Wanting to give the episode the authority of an eye witness, John, in narrating the calling of Peter and the change of name, notes: 'It was about the tenth hour' (John 1:39).

In March 2000, His Holiness John Paul II visited these holy places. It was an intense and deeply significant moment, rich in Biblical resonances. All those present remembered John the Baptist and his summons to conversion, the call recorded in the marvellous pages of John's gospel (1:35–51). Peter, in the person of his successor John Paul II, returned, for the first time in history, to the place where he had met Christ, and where Christ had looked him in the eyes and said:

> 'You are Simon, the son of John, but you will
> be called Cephas, which means Peter: a rock.'
> (John 1:42)

A few hundred metres from the ruins of Bethany beyond the Jordan, near the place where Jesus was baptised, His Holiness prayed:

> *'Glory to you, O Father, God of Abraham,*
> *Isaac and Jacob:*
> *you have sent your servants and prophets to speak*
> *to the world of your faithful love and call your*
> *people to conversion.*
> *On the banks of the river Jordan,*
> *you raised John the Baptist,*
> *a voice crying in the wilderness,*
> *and sent him throughout the region of the Jordan*
> *to prepare the way of the Lord,*
> *and announce the coming of Jesus.*
>
> *Glory to you, O Christ, Son of God:*
> *you came to the waters of the Jordan,*
> *to be baptised at the hands of John.*
> *Over you the Holy Spirit rose as a dove:*

above you the heavens opened,
and the voice of the Father was heard:
'This is my dearest son.'
In the river blessed by your presence, you went to
be baptised not only with water but with the fire of
the Holy Spirit.

Glory to you, O Holy Spirit,
Lord and giver of life:
with your strength the Church is baptised,
descending with Christ to death and rising again
with him to new life.'

Pilgrimage of 45,000
Jordanian Christians
to the site of Jesus'
Baptism, during the
Jubilee of 2000. It
was the largest
gathering of
Jordanian Christians
for many centuries.

Christianity in Jordan through the centuries

To have an overview of Christianity in Jordan, it is important to remember the geographical and Biblical background of the story of salvation, and to return to the story of the prophets, Christ, the Apostles, the martyrs and the saints.

The Christians of Jordan are the heirs of the civilisations mentioned in the Bible. Their Christian identity is inextricably linked to the holy places and to the history of the Church in the Middle East, especially in the Holy Land.

Christianity spread to Jordan from its earliest days. Eusebius of Caesarea writes that in the year 68 AD, before the destruction of Jerusalem by the Roman general Titus, the Christians of that city moved to Pella and the surrounding region, which means that there was a Christian presence in Jordan

Stadium of Amman, March 21st 2000. Solemn mass celebrated by John Paul II. Presentation of gifts from Jordanian Christians.

as early as the first century. By the end of the fourth century, Jordan was completely Christian.

The Romans had divided Palestine into three parts: *first Palestine* with Caesarea as its capital, *second Palestine*, with Beisan (Scythopolis) as its capital and important centres such as Umm Qais and Tabaqat Fahl (Pella); *third Palestine* with Petra as its capital. This administrative division remained in place until the time of the Arab conquest.

Many local tribes embraced Christianity, especially the tribes of the Ghassasina in the central northern part of the country and the Nabataeans in the south. In many places, Christianity adopted the tribal lifestyle of the people. Each tribe elected a bishop to minister to the people's spiritual needs, to educate them and strengthen them in the Christian virtues.

Between the fifth and sixth centuries the Christians built many churches, the ruins of which can still be seen today. They are a clear indication of the prosperity of the Christians, and their piety, faith and generosity. The Christians, with their strong, determined faith, were living stones in the Church of God. Out of love for their country, they competed among themselves in building churches and monasteries in every village. Monastic life and the life of hermits flourished.

Prosperity was also linked to political stability and the security of the borders, which were well defended against the Arab tribes of the desert.

After the Arab conquest, the Muslim minority and the Christian majority lived side by side. The Muslims grew in number while the Christians gradually diminished. This happened for many reasons: political and economic circumstances, social difficulties and, in some case, the threats of local rulers.

A few towns and villages like Shatana, Ermemin and Fuheis maintained their totally Christian identity until the middle of the twentieth century.

Smakieh, southern Jordan. Procession on the feast day of the Jordanian martyrs. June 2000.

Today, despite large-scale emigration since the 1950s, there are about 170,000 Christians in Jordan. They belong to various Christian denominations and rites. There are Orthodox Christians, Catholics following the Latin rite, Melchites, Maronites, Armenians, Syriacs and Chaldeans, Anglicans, Lutherans and members of other Protestant denominations.

They each maintain their own faith as part of the universal Church and strive to protect their own Arab-Christian inheritance.

Now that Christianity and Islam find themselves confronting the challenge of the changes brought about by the times, the various denominations are trying to move forward in unity, and to avoid the risks of breaking up into warring factions.

There is also an attempt to cultivate peace and harmony with their Muslim brothers, despite the

The Latin Patriarch of Jerusalem, surrounded by bishops of the Catholic churches of the Holy Land (Jordan, Palestine and Israel). Conclusion of the diocesan Synod. February 2000.

difference in their creeds. Everyone wants to embrace the most significant aspects of pluralism, appreciating the human and cultural values which both Muslims and Christians bear within themselves, and finding common ground in these values to build a future of peace and prosperity.

Even today, Christianity makes an incalculable contribution to the life of the country. Every year

Ermenim, a Jordanian village whose Latin parish was founded in 1872. The mosque is very close to the church. A positive sign of mutual friendship and respect.

thousands of people, most of them non-Christians, pass through Christian schools, hospitals, clinics and professional centres throughout Jordan, benefiting from charitable work passed on to them in the name of Christ and carrying away with them a true picture of the Gospel message, which has been demonstrated to them in deeds rather than in words.

In this sense, Jordan, too, is a 'holy land' and bears its own particular message of universal brotherhood, peaceful co-existence and mutual respect.

Appendix

The following telephone numbers are for the benefit
of groups wishing to linger and reflect or to
celebrate the Eucharist in one of the Latin parishes
of Jordan:

I. North Jordan

Irbid: S. Georgii Mart.	Tel: 02/7272314
Hosson : Conceptionis	
Immaculatae B.M.V.	Tel: 02/7010010
Khirbeh: S. Eliae Prophetae	Tel: 02/6466002
Ajlun: Ss. Petri e Pauli	Tel: 02/6421406
Anjara: Visitatio B.V.M.	Tel: 02/6461013

II. Amman

Marka: Soll. B.V.M.	
Matris Ecclesiae	Tel: 06/4883232
Loueibdeh: Soll.	
Annuntiationis B.V.M.	Tel: 06/4637440
Jabal Amman: S. Josepf Opificis	Tel: 06/4624590
Hasmini: B.V.M. de Monte Carmelo	Tel: 06/4918548
Misdar: D.N.J.C. universorum Regis	Tel: 06/4772623
Tila El Ali: S. Cordis Jesu	Tel: 06/5519807
Sweifiyeh: B.V.M. de Nazareth	Tel: 06/5920740
Jabal Hussain: S. Joannis de La Salle	Tel: 06/5661757

III. Southern Jordan

Madaba: Passio S. Joannis Baptistae	Tel: 05/3244065
Mount Nebo	Tel; 05/3252938
Karak: B.V.M. a Rosario	Tel: 03/2352337
Ader: Ss. Angelorum Custodum	Tel: 03/2380775
Smakieh: S. Michael Archang.	Tel: 03/2320152
Aqaba (Sisters of the Rosary)	Tel: 03/2014260

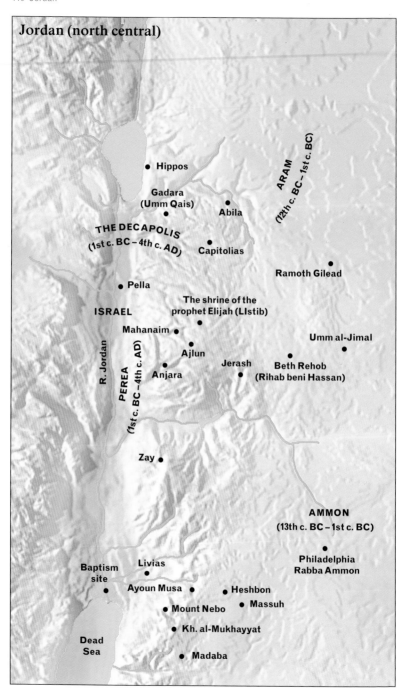

Jordan (north central)

ARAM
(12th c. BC – 1st c. BC)

Hippos

Gadara
(Umm Qais)

Abila

THE DECAPOLIS
(1st c. BC – 4th c. AD)

Capitolias

Ramoth Gilead

Pella

The shrine of the
prophet Elijah (LIstib)

ISRAEL

Mahanaim

Umm al-Jimal

Ajlun

R. Jordan

Jerash

Anjara

Beth Rehob
(Rihab beni Hassan)

PEREA
(1st c. BC – 4th c. AD)

Zay

AMMON
(13th c. BC – 1st c. BC)

Baptism
site

Livias

Philadelphia
Rabba Ammon

Ayoun Musa

Heshbon

Mount Nebo

Massuh

Kh. al-Mukhayyat

Dead
Sea

Madaba

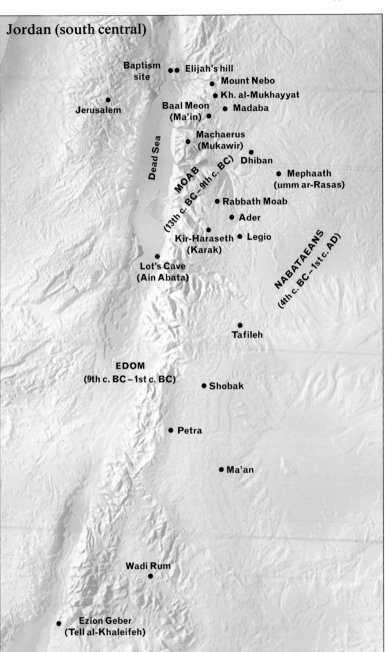

Jordan (south central)

Baptism
site

Elijah's hill

Mount Nebo

Kh. al-Mukhayyat

Jerusalem

Baal Meon
(Ma'in)

Madaba

Dead Sea

Machaerus
(Mukawir)

MOAB
(13th c. BC – 9th c. BC)

Dhiban

Mephaath
(umm ar-Rasas)

Rabbath Moab

Ader

Kir-Haraseth
(Karak)

Legio

NABATAEANS
(4th c. BC – 1st c. AD)

Lot's Cave
(Ain Abata)

Tafileh

EDOM
(9th c. BC – 1st c. BC)

Shobak

Petra

Ma'an

Wadi Rum

Ezion Geber
(Tell al-Khaleifeh)

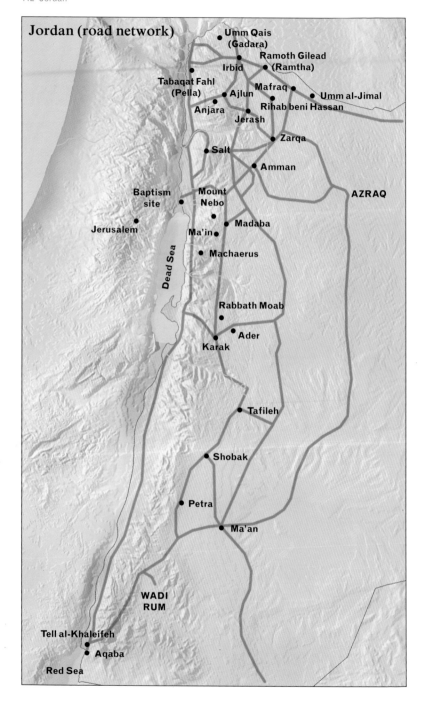

Jordan (road network)

Umm Qais (Gadara)
Ramoth Gilead (Ramtha)
Irbid
Tabaqat Fahl (Pella)
Mafraq
Umm al-Jimal
Ajlun
Anjara
Rihab beni Hassan
Jerash
Zarqa
Salt
Amman
Baptism site
Mount Nebo
AZRAQ
Jerusalem
Madaba
Ma'in
Dead Sea
Machaerus
Rabbath Moab
Ader
Karak
Tafileh
Shobak
Petra
Ma'an
WADI RUM
Tell al-Khaleifeh
Aqaba
Red Sea